MW00346060

PORSCHE 911

Other Titles in the Crowood AutoClassics Series

PORSCHE 911
The Complete Story
David Vivian

First published in 1990 by
The Crowood Press Ltd
Ramsbury, Marlborough
Wiltshire SN8 2HR

This impression 1997

British Library Cataloguing-in-Publication Data

Vivian, David 1956 –
   Porsche 911.
   1. Porsche 911 cars, history
   I. Title
   629.2′222

   ISBN 1 85223 330 3

The photographs in this book were kindly supplied by The
Motoring Picture Library, Beaulieu; with the exception of those
on pages 60, 61, 116, 124-5, 129, 144, 156-7, 165 (bottom), 177
and 189 (top) which are reproduced courtesy of *Autocar & Motor*;
those on pages 161, 164 and 165 (top) which are reproduced
courtesy of Autofarm Ltd; and those on pages 8-9 and 21 which
are reproduced courtesy of Dr. Ing. h.c.F. Porsche AG.

The line-drawings that appear on pages 50, 52 and 55 were
drawn by Terry Hunns.

Printed and bound in Great Britain by
The Bath Press, Bath

Contents

To Sarah-Lindsay

Acknowledgements

When The Crowood Press first approached me to write a book for its *AutoClassics* series, the car it had lined up was the Lamborghini Countach. Excited as I was by the prospect of contributing to a new publishing venture, I couldn't accept the commission. The last thing I'd written about the Lamborghini had to be vetted by a lawyer. The more I drove the Countach the less I liked it. Perverse maybe, but true.

My old friend and one-time colleague Peter Dron, however, was more of a fan and offered to take the 'problem child' under his wing while I thought again. I now realise that choosing the 911 was a lot braver than it seemed at the time. This is not a lightweight subject and only now do I know how little I knew before I started. Special thanks are due to Michael Cotton, Chris Harvey, Paul Frère and Karl Ludvigsen for having trodden this path before and for having forged a clearing through the tangle of facts that is the 911's history.

Thanks are also due to Jeremy Snook and Corinna Phillips at Porsche GB and to those at Porsche's Zuffenhausen HQ whom I have pestered for old press releases and charts.

Finally, apologies to Guy and Anna at The Crowood Press for keeping them waiting so long for the 'difficult' chapters in this book. Many thanks for being so patient and understanding.

David Vivian
October 1989

THE 911 FAMILY TREE – FROM 1969 2-LITRE 911 COUPE TO 1988 959

959 Coupé
1987–1988, 2848 ccm, 450 PS

961 Coupé
1986–1987, 2847 ccm, 680 PS

911 SC/RS Coupé
1984, 2994 ccm, 255 PS

935/78 Turbo Coupé »Moby Dick«
1978, 3211 ccm, 750 PS

935 Turbo Coupé
1976–1977, 2857 ccm, 590/630 PS

959 Coupé »Paris–Dakar«
1985–1986, 2847 ccm, 400 PS

911 Carrera 4 x 4 Coupé »Paris–Dakar«
1984, 3164 ccm, 225 PS

911 SC Coupé »Safari«
1978, 2994 ccm, 250 PS

934 Turbo Coupé
1976–1977, 2994 ccm, 485 PS

911 Carrera 4 Coupé
ab 1989, 3557 ccm, 250 PS

935 Turbo Coupé »Baby«
1977, 1425 ccm, 320 PS

911 Turbo (3.3) Cabrio
ab 1986, 3299 ccm, 300 PS

911 Turbo (3.3) Targa
ab 1986, 3299 ccm, 300 PS

911 Turbo (3.3) Coupé
ab 1978, 3299 ccm, 300 PS

911 Carrera (3.2) Cabrio
ab 1984, 3164 ccm, 231 PS

911 Carrera (3.2) Coupé
ab 1984, 3164 ccm, 231 PS

911 SC Cabrio
1982–1983, 2994 ccm, 204 PS

911 SC Coupé
1981–1983, 2994 ccm, 204 PS

911 SC Targa
1980, 2994 ccm, 188 PS

911 SC Targa
1978–1980, 2994 ccm, 180 PS

911 Carrera 3.0 Coupé
1976–1977, 2994 ccm, 200 PS

911 Speedster
ab 1989, 3164 ccm, 231 PS

1989							
1988							
1987							
1986							
1985							
1984							
1983							
1982							
1981							
1980							
1979							
1978							
1977							
1976							

PORSCHE

Dr. Ing. h. c. F. Porsche AG · Stuttgart-Zuffenhausen · Printed in Germany · WVK 351 310

Modell-jahr

'75
- 911 Turbo (3.0) Coupé 1975-1977, 2994 ccm, 260 PS
- 911 S - 2.7 Coupé 1974-1977, 2687 ccm, 175 PS
- 911 E - 2.7 Targa 1974-1977, 2687 ccm, 150 PS
- 912 E Coupé 1976, 1971 ccm, 90 PS

1974
- 911 Carrera RSR Turbo Coupé 1974, 2142 ccm, 500 PS (22)
- 911 Carrera RS 3.0 Coupé 1974, 2994 ccm, 230 PS
- 911 Carrera 2.7 Coupé 1974-1975, 2687 ccm, 210 PS

1973
- 911 Carrera RSR 3.0 1973-1974, 2994 ccm, 315/330 PS (51 GT)
- 911 Carrera RSR 2.8 Coupé 1973, 2806 ccm, 300 PS (8)
- 911 Carrera RS 2.7 Coupé 1973, 2687 ccm, 210 PS
- 911 S - 2.4 Coupé 1972-1973, 2341 ccm, 190 PS
- 911 T - 2.4 Targa 1972-1973, 2341 ccm, 130 PS
- 911 E - 2.4 Coupé 1972-1973, 2341 ccm, 165 PS

1972
- 911 S - 2.5 Coupé 1972, 2492 ccm, 270 PS (25)
- 911 S - 2.2 Coupé »Safari« 1971, 2195 ccm, 180 PS (19)

1971
- 911 Carrera 2.7 Coupé 1974-1975, 2687 ccm, 210 PS
- 911 T - 2.2 Targa 1970-1971, 2195 ccm, 125 PS
- 911 S - 2.2 Coupé 1970-1971, 2195 ccm, 180 PS
- 911 T - 2.2 Coupé 1970-1971, 2195 ccm, 155 PS

1970
- 911 S - 2.3 Coupé 1970, 2247 ccm, 240 PS (59)
- 911 S - 2.2 Coupé »Rallye« 1970, 2195 ccm, 180 PS (6)
- 911 S - 2.4 Coupé »Proto« 1970, 2395 ccm, 260 PS (139)

'69

'68
- 911 T (2.0) Coupé 1968-1969, 1991 ccm, 110 PS
- 911 S (2.0) Coupé 1967-1969, 1991 ccm, 160 PS
- 911 E (2.0) Coupé 1969, 1991 ccm, 140 PS
- 911 L (2.0) Coupé 1968, 1991 ccm, 130 PS

'67
- 911 R (2.0) Coupé 1967, 1991 ccm, 210 PS (181)
- 911 S (2.0) Coupé »Rallye« 1967, 1991 ccm, 170 PS (41)
- 911 (2.0) Targa 1967, 1991 ccm, 130 PS

'66 / '65
- 911 (2.0) Coupé »Monte« 1965, 1991 ccm, 160 PS (147)
- 911 (2.0) Coupé 1965-1967, 1991 ccm, 130 PS
- 912 Coupé 1965-1969, 1582 ccm, 90 PS

1964

1963
- 901 Coupé 1963, 1991 ccm, 130 PS

Introduction

The only justification I would claim for this, a new book about Porsche's 911, is that it was written out of real interest in the car. If the reader asks how I may presume to undertake such a work having never owned even one 911 – unlike those who have owned many – I can only point out that as a motoring writer working on weekly magazines for the past twelve years, I've driven more than a few and have always been stimulated and fascinated by the experience.

The stories of some of the encounters appear in the book and express closely the feelings and opinions I held at the time. It would be wrong to pretend that they haven't changed in the ensuing years. The 911 is an easy car to 'fall out of love' with, especially for a magazine writer who is constantly

Unforgettable. The shape that launched a legend – the 356. This one was built in 1949, a year before full production. The 911 wasn't to follow for another fifteen years.

911: TWENTY SIX YEARS OF EVOLUTION

1963   The story starts with the prototype 901. A bigger and more sophisticated version of the original Volkswagen-based Porsche 356 dating from 1947, the 901 is launched at the Frankfurt Motor Show to a fascinated and enthusiastic public. Created by Porsche founder's son, Ferry, and styled by grandson, Butzi, the 911 incarnate has some engineering input from nephew Ferdinand Piech. It's a family affair.

1964   With a dry-sump, air-cooled 1,991cc flat-six engine developing 130bhp, the '901' enters production, its proud makers oblivious to the fact that Peugeot has registered trademark numbers with zero in the middle. The French car maker is outraged and Porsche is forced to rename its sports car '911'.

1965   For the first and, perhaps, the only time, the 911's development is influenced by a British trend. A targa-topped variant, inspired by the optional hardtop on the Triumph TR sports cars, is introduced. Also in this year, the 911's appeal is targeted down market with the entry-level 912 model. This uses the old 356 four-cylinder engine.

1966   The notorious 911S bows in. Its peaky high-performance engine develops an impressive 160bhp.

1967   911 range becomes more clearly delineated with base 110bhp 911T for touring, 130bhp 911L for luxury and 911S and 210bhp 911R for racing. Controversial semi-automatic transmission – dubbed 'Sportomatic' – is introduced but aimed primarily at US market.

1968   Rim width is increased from 4.5in (11.4cm) to 5.5in (14cm) as a prelude to more significant chassis changes.

1969   The career-long amelioration of the 911's tricky cornering balance starts here with a 2.24in (5.7cm) extension of the wheelbase. Diesel-style mechanical fuel injection invigorates 911E (which replaces 911L) and revised 911S. Suspension and tyre options diverge to accommodate different requirements and tastes. The 'comfort' approach is provided by 14in (35.5cm) wheels and self-levelling dampers while those with a more sporting inclination can opt for 15in (38cm) wheels with wider 6in (15cm) rims. The boxy mid-engined 914 is conceived as a keenly-priced Porsche to replace the 912 but ends up costing the same as the 911 once VW has taken its slice of the profits from body building. This, in turn, forces up the price of the 911.

1970   A hike in capacity to 2,195cc brings power increases across the board: 125bhp for the 911T, 155bhp for the 911E and 180bhp for the 911S. A 911ST rally version is launched.

1971   911's reputation for longevity and durability is sired in this year with the introduction of significant body sections made from corrosion-resistant galvanised steel.

1972   The quest for power continues with the flat-six growing to 2,341cc. This gives 130bhp for the 911TV, 140bhp for the 911TE, 165bhp for the 911E and 190bhp for the ever-more exciting 911S. The old gearbox, with first out on a back-left dog-leg, is replaced with a conventional-pattern change transmission. Under Piech's guidance, the development programme has become almost obsessive: an oil reservoir is moved a few centimetres at great expense to give more even weight distribution. The Porsche dynasty divides. Ferry Porsche remains in charge but Ferdinand Piech and Butzi Porsche go their separate ways.

1973   The fabulous Carrera RS – maybe the best 911 of all – makes its debut. Produced in 2,687cc, 210bhp Touring or Lightweight guises with optional ducktail spoiler and 7in (17.7cm) wide rear wheels, it's soon followed by a wide-wheeled 315bhp version and a 330bhp RSR racer.

1974   The ominous spectre of US safety legislation forces Porsche to fit big bumpers to the 911, the weight inevitably goes up and so 2.7-litre capacity is standardised. To comply with stiffer exhaust emission regulations, electronic fuel injection is introduced. This blunts the responsiveness of the 150bhp 911 and the 175bhp 911S but makes them both more fuel-efficient. RS evolves into 210bhp Carrera and retains mechanical injection for European markets but gets 911S engine for US. High performance 911s are still in great demand and Porsche produces a limited run of Carrera 3.0RS (2,994cc, 230–330bhp) and 2,143cc turbo RSR racers.

1975   Fuel crisis blues depress sports car sales but merely spur Porsche on to greater things. This is the year of the wide-bodied, 260bhp 911 Turbo – officially 930 – which essentially adds a turbocharger, luxury equipment pack and tea-tray aerofoil to the basic Carrera 3.0RS specification. Turbo has higher top speed (around 155mph (249kph)) and, thanks to shorter trailing arms at the back and new ultra low-profile Pirelli P7 tyres, better handling. Porsche introduces front-engined, water-cooled 924.

1976   911 bodyshell is now completely galvanised and allows Porsche to offer an unprecedented six-year anti-corrosion guarantee. Model line up comprises 2.7-litre 165bhp 911, 200bhp electronic injection 3-litre Carrera 3 (still called 911S in the US) and the Turbo. Unsurprisingly, Turbo spawns more muscular versions for racing – the 450bhp 934 and the still more spectacular 2,856cc, 630bhp 935 with its superlight bodywork. What is surprising is that suave new 928 grand tourer fails to put a dent in 911 sales.

1977   The range now reads 911, 911 Lux, Carrera 3, Carrera 3 Sport (with Turbo's uprated running gear) and Turbo. In racing, 935s are developing between 370bhp from 1,425cc to 630bhp from a twin-turbo 3,211cc 77A model.

1978   Carrera 3 loses its hard-edged character to become 911SC with 180bhp (166bhp in US) but Turbo gets both heavier and more powerful, its 3,299cc engine delivering 300bhp (265bhp in US). The bigger engine sits further back, creating potential handling problems but bigger brakes are fitted to cope with the extra performance (160+mph (257kph)). Diversification is back with a bang and 911SC is offered with Turbo wings and wheels as a sort of 'poor man's look-alike' but some critics actually prefer it to the often unforgiving real thing. Few genuine or important developments this year, though. On the track, four-valve water-cooled heads for 935 extract an awesome 750bhp. (35/78 gets 936 bodywork.)

1979   Stunning aerodynamics help 935K3 win the Le Mans 24 Hours. Continuing to receive rave reviews from the motoring press, the 928 isn't impressing 911 customers who go on buying their favourite Porsche. 911SC gets 188bhp (180bhp in US).

1980   Porsche buying public's clear preference for 911 over 928 is beginning to cause concern and embarrassment in Zuffenhausen's corridors of power. Porsche chief Ernst Fuhrmann attempts to kill off 911 to boost 928 sales but fails and is replaced by American Peter Schutz who is briefed by Ferry Porsche to revamp the 911.

1981   The Schutz influence is quickly apparent as 911SC power is increased to 204bhp Extravagantly expensive 'flat nose' 911 styled along the lines of the four-wheel drive cabriolet prototype is shown at the Frankfurt Show.

1982   911SC Cabriolet is unveiled at the Geneva Show. It is the first true convertible Porsche since the 356. Meanwhile the success of the 944 is putting the skids under the future of the car that spawned it, the 924.

1983   The Carrera is back and the SC out. The bigger (3,164cc) engine develops 231bhp (200bhp in US and Japan) but is more fuel-efficient, too. The Super Sport is born – essentially a Turbo in body, chassis, brakes and tyres but with the normally-aspirated Carrera engine. Dramatically-styled Group B show car points the way for 911 development.

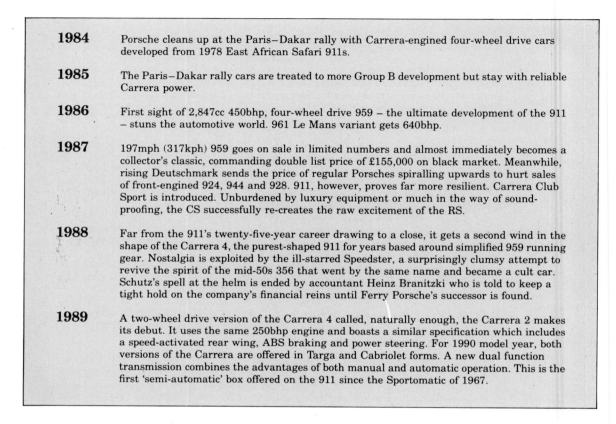

1984	Porsche cleans up at the Paris–Dakar rally with Carrera-engined four-wheel drive cars developed from 1978 East African Safari 911s.
1985	The Paris–Dakar rally cars are treated to more Group B development but stay with reliable Carrera power.
1986	First sight of 2,847cc 450bhp, four-wheel drive 959 – the ultimate development of the 911 – stuns the automotive world. 961 Le Mans variant gets 640bhp.
1987	197mph (317kph) 959 goes on sale in limited numbers and almost immediately becomes a collector's classic, commanding double list price of £155,000 on black market. Meanwhile, rising Deutschmark sends the price of regular Porsches spiralling upwards to hurt sales of front-engined 924, 944 and 928. 911, however, proves far more resilient. Carrera Club Sport is introduced. Unburdened by luxury equipment or much in the way of sound-proofing, the CS successfully re-creates the raw excitement of the RS.
1988	Far from the 911's twenty-five-year career drawing to a close, it gets a second wind in the shape of the Carrera 4, the purest-shaped 911 for years based around simplified 959 running gear. Nostalgia is exploited by the ill-starred Speedster, a surprisingly clumsy attempt to revive the spirit of the mid-50s 356 that went by the same name and became a cult car. Schutz's spell at the helm is ended by accountant Heinz Branitzki who is told to keep a tight hold on the company's financial reins until Ferry Porsche's successor is found.
1989	A two-wheel drive version of the Carrera 4 called, naturally enough, the Carrera 2 makes its debut. It uses the same 250bhp engine and boasts a similar specification which includes a speed-activated rear wing, ABS braking and power steering. For 1990 model year, both versions of the Carrera are offered in Targa and Cabriolet forms. A new dual function transmission combines the advantages of both manual and automatic operation. This is the first 'semi-automatic' box offered on the 911 since the Sportomatic of 1967.

having to assess general standards and re-assess his own. But then the 911 has never depended on critical approval to sustain its phenomenal success. And it's hard to stay angry with it for long. Like the scariest ride at a fairground, the 911 has a magnetic attraction for anyone with even a trace of adventure in their blood.

The obvious question to ask is how this small and not very pretty sportscar has been able to resist the sort of violent consumer mood swings and burgeoning political press-ures that have crushed some contemporary designs clean out of the running?

It is not, I believe, because the 911 is a good car. By definition, 'good' cars tend to be all virtue and no vice and the 911 has never been that. Almost the opposite. The 'nine-eleven' has the toughest maverick streak of any car in production. If there is anything genuinely pure in the car's make-up – and enthusiasts contend that it represents driv-ing in its purest form – it was conceived when straight line speed was the only virtue worth talking about, and never mind the finer nuances of handling balance.

That didn't mean just having the engine behind the driver, of course, but way back in the boot – no different to the little 356 that preceded the 911 and the ever so humble VW Beetle that preceded the 356.

Our story starts even before that: with the family history, and in particular, the young Ferdinand Porsche. My main intention with this book has been to provide a balanced account of the 911, which must include some background and perspective as well as the 'I was there' driving experiences. I have

Porsche 356 Sprint (1959).

*The family 911, a dynasty spanning twenty-six years. From
right to left: 2-litre 911 Coupe from 1965, 3-litre 911 Turbo from
1975 and the mighty 2.9-litre, all-drive 959 from 1988, maybe
the greatest supercar of all.*

911 Carrera Club Sport – a reincarnation of the purist's 911 typified by the Carrera RS.

Unquestionably one of the great motoring experiences – classic Porsche plus wind-in-the-hair equals 911 Carrera Cabriolet.

'Tea tray' spoiler became a mildly controversial feature of later high-performance 911s.

admiration for the 'established' 911 authors: the extraordinary technical insight and thoroughness of Paul Frère; the pointillist observations and easy understanding of Michael Cotton, the effortless and lightly-borne knowledge of Chris Harvey. By covering a lot of ground in a relatively short space, I've tried to make this big subject a little more digestible or, at the very least, worth tasting.

At the time of writing this introduction, the 911's future is the subject of speculation once more. The remarkable Panamericana styling exercise – based around Carrera 4 mechanicals – has just received a mixed reception at the 1989 Frankfurt Show. Porsche says it represents *an* approach the 911 may yet take. I'm not alone in thinking it looks like a beach buggy. Whatever the outcome, we can assume that the 911 will be around for some time yet and there'll always be people who want to write about it.

1 Roots

Like a master storyteller's innate ability to spin out a simple plot while retaining the listener's undivided attention, Porsche has commanded the similarly special knack of stretching an old design over the span of decades without diminishing its popularity.

The seemingly immortal 911 is a design which, almost incredibly, can trace its roots back to the Beetle-esque flat-four engined 356 yet which today, as the Carrera 4, is widely acknowledged as not only one of the world's most capable supercars but also one of the most practical and useable day-to-day. This in spite of a rear-engined chassis configuration that, by all rights, should have been dead and buried before Neil Armstrong set foot upon the moon. For Porsche, however, the 911's story has yet to enter its final chapter.

Its creator was born in 1875 in Maffersdorf, Bohemia. His name was Ferdinand Porsche. A child with obvious inventive flair and more than a little manual dexterity, the young Porsche devised and installed a system of electric lighting in the family home that left the rest of the neighbourhood in the dark ages. He was sixteen.

Progress from bright kid to car maker was swift. Aged twenty-five, Ferdinand Porsche exhibited his first crack at personal transport, the electric hub-driven Lohner Porsche, at the Paris show. The first production model was sold to Luton resident Mr E W Hart. This may have been an early sign of Porsche's penchant for private enterprise, but the young Bohemian wasn't ready to go it alone just yet . . .

As early as 1910, Dr Ferdinand Porsche had already confronted the problem of wind resistance. On his seventy-fifth birthday, only a few months before his death, he recollects:

'At that time, in order to achieve good performance, engines had to run at a very high revolution rate: around 2,800rpm. It quickly became clear that it wasn't possible to make the engines of the day rev any higher and I would now have to look at the problem from another angle. That's when I thought of wind resistance. So I streamlined the wings, the axles and the headlamps and was able to establish that an enormous build up in speed resulted.'

Ferdinand Porsche's eldest son, 'Ferry' Porsche, confirms his father's perfectionist streak. 'It was in my father's nature that he was never satisfied with what he had achieved. The richness of his ideas was inexhaustible. His motto was – every problem that is set to a person is solvable.'

Technical directorship of the Austrian Daimler company in Stuttgart came to Dr Ferdinand Porsche in 1924. With D–B, he was directly responsible for several landmark Mercedes–Benz designs, including the 'S' and 'SSK' supercharged cars.

MORE THAN VALUABLE EXPERIENCE

In 1931, Dr Ferdinand Porsche established his own design office for engine and vehicle construction in Stuttgart. Outside contracts were soon on the table, the first of which would lead to the design and manufacture of

356 production went from 1950 (though the first example was built in 1948) to 1965 when the 911 was introduced. This is an A type, made in 1957.

Pedigree

1963–1988 25 Years of the Porsche 911

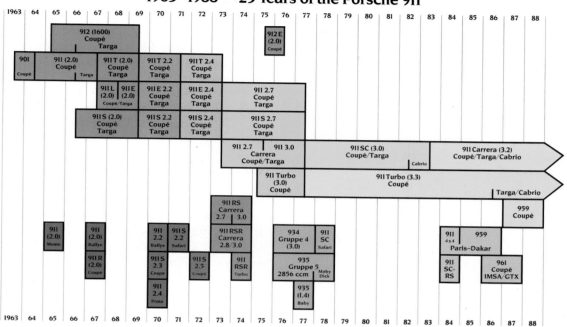

Twenty-five year pedigree line of 911. The golden years are actually marked in green: memorable models include RS Carrera, RSR and 935 Gruppe 5 (also known as Moby Dick).

a six-cylinder passenger car for Wanderer. The project that followed, however, turned out to be a far more pertinent signpost to the future – a brief to design and build a Grand Prix car for Auto Union.

Much of the early test work for this rear-engined V16 leviathan was undertaken by son Ferry Porsche, and its success in battling the redoubtable Mercedes–Benz Grand Prix cars on the circuits of Europe pointed not only to the effectiveness of the advanced torsion bar suspension but to Ferry's skill as an engineer.

By 1939, however, dark clouds were forming over Europe and, with the outbreak of World War II, Stuttgart became a bombing target. Porsche moved operations to Austria where, in the summer of 1948, a car that was to make automotive history was given its first test drive. In the yard of a former saw

mill, the first car created by and to bear the name of 'Porsche' saw the light of day. This was, quite literally, car 'no 1' – an open two-seater carrying a modified VW engine sitting just ahead of the rear axle with the gearbox to the rear. A true 'mid-engined' car and forerunner to the rear-engined 356, this car is, today, a priceless exhibit in the Porsche museum. With an original thirty-five horsepower rating, car 'no 1' was capable of nearly 90mph (145kph).

ENTER THE SPORTS CAR

If the first press and public reactions to this design weren't exactly ecstatic, they were at least positive enough to encourage Porsche to build car 'no 2' – this time a compact

Butzi Porsche

A gifted stylist, Ferry Porsche's eldest son, Ferdinand Porsche III – known as 'Butzi' – first displayed his flair for design on the Formula Two racing car that had been developed alongside the 356. The first real project of his own, however, was the limited-run 904GT racing car of 1963. There's no denying Butzi's most famous shape, though: the 911.

In his formative years, Butzi loved drawing houses and wanted to be an architect. Today, he runs Porsche Design, a studio with just a dozen staff near the family home in Zell am Zee, Austria. And *design* is the operative word.

Apart from the famous Porsche Design range of sunglasses, watches and ashtrays, Butzi's genius has touched products as diverse NEC's standard telephone and Kandido interior lighting; Yashica's Contax T camera and the Kineo motor yacht. Simplicity and purity of line – that's the magic that binds these products.

Butzi remains a very private man and lives in a 15th century castle with his wife and three children.

coupe with a dome-shaped roof and the engine shifted to behind the rear axle to make space for luggage and an extra seat. Model 356 was born.

Ferry Porsche explained:

'From the beginning we envisaged a small sports car with which you could cover long distances without tiring the driver and co-driver. This idea couldn't be exploited because it didn't fit in with the national political policy of the time. Three years after moving to Gmund in 1944, drawings were made for a sports car based on the VW Beetle. The greatest part of our equipment had been lost in the war. Hardly any financial means were at hand, yet we were able to produce fifty high quality cars in the twelve months between 1948 and 1949. All were hand made, reflecting the quality for which we were soon to become world renowned.'

In 1949, the Porsche team returned to Stuttgart. One year later, volume production of the 356 commenced. The model started out with an 1,100cc, 40bhp engine. Over the next fifteen years, the phased up-rating for which Porsche has become famous saw 1,300, 1,500 and, eventually, 1,600cc versions, the latter developing 95bhp.

The shape of the 356, styled in its coupe form by Erwin Kommenda, was hailed as one of alluring beauty. Critics raved about its overt sleekness and daring technical specification and, perhaps most important of all, of a 'new driving experience'.

Private drivers soon discovered the 356's suitability as a sports racing car. A Porsche appeared as a works entry for the first time at the 1951 Le Mans 24 Hours race with a 1,100cc coupe. In truth, there was no greater test for a first outing and, with a flair that was to become monotonous through repetition, the Porsche won its class convincingly.

THE WILL TO WIN

Soon Porsche was designing cars specially for racing. In 1953, the company built the 550 – as a spider or, for fast circuits, a coupe. The 1,500cc air-cooled engine that powered the 550 was to become world famous and Porsche's most potent weapon in motorsport for almost a decade.

Externally similar to the other Porsche spiders, the 550 entered for the 1953 German Grand Prix had a strikingly different sound. It was the sound of the 1.5-litre 'Carrera' engine, a high-output unit that had been developed in secret and one that could easily be enlarged to 2 litres. It had four overhead camshafts, was king-shaft driven and, initially, developed 110bhp.

Sportscar for the family man, the 1956–1957 356 Carrera GT Coupe.

1959 Speedster convertible was, perhaps, the most elegant 356 of all. Few were made, it is now a rare classic.

Ferdinand Piech

A year younger than Butzi Porsche, Ferdinand Piech was nicknamed 'Burli' or *little boy*. A talented and ambitious engineer who had started work, in 1963, on the development of the flat-six engine and five-speed transmission that ultimately found its way into the 911, he abandoned his research and development post during the management crisis of 1972 to go to a similar job at Audi. After sixteen years he was made chairman.

Rumours abound over who will eventually be boss at Porsche, but Piech denies any interest, explaining that his present role as one of the eight third generation family members on the firm's supervisory board suits him.

His influence at Audi has been considerable, especially his unerring support of the quattro concept and fully galvanised bodies. He believes that Audi lacks the strength of image to compete with Mercedes, BMW and Porsche but has few doubts that it's only a matter of time before the marque acquires it.

Piech is a hard and capable driver and has used a Sport quattro and a 300bhp Sport-engined 200 quattro as personal transport. He has been married three times and has twelve children. He likes to keep fit by jogging, skiing and cycling.

By 1955, the Carrera engine had become so advanced that it was ready to be slotted into a road car. That car was the 356 1500 GS. With a standard exhaust system, it achieved a remarkable 100bhp. Meanwhile, the 356 was living up to its promise as the ideal vehicle for the private racer. In the mid-fifties the smaller GT classes were often dominated by Porsche 356s with either Carrera or pushrod engines. The only real concession to the track environment was the use of open Sebring exhaust systems.

As the 356 improved each year, the difference between it and the VW Beetle became more and more apparent. The racing success of the Carrera engine grew greater too, until, in 1956, Porsche achieved its first overall victory – the long distance endurance race at the Targa Florio in Italy.

Formula Two rules were changed in 1957 and it was good news for the Stuttgart factory, with the new maximum capacity for the formula set at 1.5 litres, success was as inevitable as it was swift. In the 1960 German Grand Prix, where only Formula Two cars were accepted, Porsche so dominated the race with its 190bhp cars, that it took 1st, 2nd, 4th, 5th and 6th places. But for Jack Brabham's 3rd place in a Cooper–Climax, it would have been a Porsche clean-sweep. To no one's great surprise, Porsche won the Constructors World Championship for Formula Two cars that year.

SINGULAR SUCCESS

Porsche's growing stature in single-seater racing was confirmed in 1961 when a change of rules gave the company a crack at Formula One, the most competitive and prestigious class in motor racing. The formula had just been re-defined, the previous 2.5-litre capacity limit dropping to 1.5 litres. For once, though, Porsche's four-cylinder engine was well off the pace.

In the spring of 1962, the car that was to mark a change of fortunes, albeit short-lived, rolled out of the factory. It was powered by a flat-eight engine with 180bhp and tipped the scales at just 980lbs (444kg). In 1962, Dan Gurney won the French Grand Prix with this car. It was to be its only victory. At the end of 1962, Porsche withdrew from Formula One altogether.

Back with sports car racing, the proven 4-cylinder Carrera engine, now with a 2-litre

(Right): *356 Super 90 (1959) was powered by 90bhp flat-four engine and capable of 110mph.*

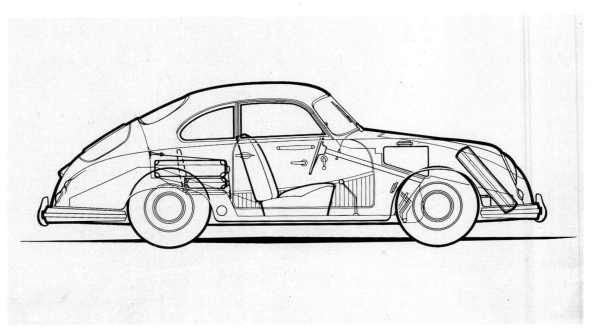

Simple schematic of 356 shows basic design principles that were
followed through to 911: boot and spare wheel in the front,
engine in the back and plenty of space for two.

356A convertible managed 98mph from just 60bhp and 1.6
litres. This is a 1958 model.

A 356A among the cars that inspired its design – Volkswagen's ubiquitous Beetle.

capacity (185bhp) and powering the successor to the 550, the model 718, had reached its peak. It was replaced by two versions of the Formula One engine – carrying a 2-litre and 2.2-litre, respectively turning out 210 and 270bhp.

911

Meanwhile, the series production cars had reached another milestone. At the 1963 Frankfurt show, a radically new car was presented to an expectant world: the 911.

The successor to the 356 had a 2-litre 6-cylinder boxer engine producing 130bhp. Ferry Porsche relates:

'As early as 1956 we started with the plans for a new model. It was to be a comfortable touring car but, unlike the 356, parts from the large-series cars were not utilised as these were no longer suitable for further development.

'Various models were designed, even

(Overleaf): *Some 356s carried luggage on their backs.*

911S and T from 1968. The faster S had 170bhp and 140mph top speed.

Early 911 (1968 'L') had a purity of line that was lost with later models. Note the distinctive alloy wheels.

some with a notchback with the aim of creating a true four-seater. But finally it remained a sports car in concept, with 2+2 packaging. We didn't want to allow the Porsche shape, which had become world famous in the meantime, to disappear. As a power unit, a 6-cylinder engine was chosen. But then it occurred to me, remembering our motorsport activities, that front engines were not competitive enough on a long term basis, and so we kept to the rear engine.'

In motor racing Porsche returned with its 4-cylinder Carrera engine powering the 1964 model 904 GTS. This car, which was a two-seater mid-engined coupe, was praised for its radical design. The bodywork, for the first time, was constructed in glass fibre. Class wins came in its first races at Daytona and at Sebring.

In 1965, the 904 was replaced by the 906. With the now proven, stronger 6-cylinder engine, it developed a healthy 210bhp. Typical styling characteristics of the 906 were the gull-wing doors and the height of only 40in (101cm). Fifty cars had to be built to comply with the rules for sports cars and all were sold within only a few weeks.

No substantial engine changes were made for the 910 and 907 models which succeeded

The famous flat-six engine that has powered the 911 through two-and-a-half decades. This is a 1968 example with fuel injection.

912 was introduced as an 'entry level' 911 and used an up-rated version of the 356's flat-four engine. The facia design, however, was very similar.

the 906. All were powered by the proven 6 and 8-cylinder engines.

POWER PLAY

During the mid-60s, Porsche's spoils from motor racing consisted mostly of class wins with very few overall victories. The factory wasn't happy. Porsche's desire to succeed was absolute and that meant outright wins. Success, however, wasn't long in coming.

With the 917 and 906, Porsche won the world championship for makes from 1969 to 1971. The sports car scene conquered – for the time being at least – it was the Can–Am series' turn to feel the might of Zuffenhausen. In 1972, the awesomely powerful McLarens with their 750bhp 8-litre Chevrolet engines were dominant. Faced with the problem of creating more power, Porsche turned to something it had experimented with way back in 1939, the turbocharger. The 917 motor served as a starting point,

achieving an unbelievable 1,000bhp with the help of the exhaust-driven blower.

In 1972, Mark Donnahue and George Former took the Can–Am championship. Porsche repeated the feat in 1973, the title going to Donnahue. In the meantime, the most powerful racing machine of all was built, the 917.30. A 5.4-litre capacity delivered a staggering 1,100bhp. An example of the 917.30, one of the few built, is on show in the Porsche museum.

For the production series cars, development continued apace. From early days, the 911 had been successful in racing and rallies, but it was the Carrera that really excelled in the sport and, for many years, was virtually unbeatable in the GT category.

For 1975, the formidable 2.7-litre Carrera's capacity was increased to 3 litres with a nominal output of 210bhp, though racing versions developed up to 330bhp. Those drivers who were able to spot a winner, and there were many, switched to the Porsche and it wasn't long before the GT class up to

911s were to become a common sight at race meetings, especially the Le Mans 24 Hours. Drivers Buchet and Linge compete in the 1967 event in a 911S.

3-litres was both awash with and dominated by Carreras.

At about the same time, two new production cars made their debuts. In October 1974, Porsche introduced the 911 Turbo at the Paris Motor Show. At last, the invaluable racing experience with turbocharging had borne fruit in series production. The 3-litre 6-cylinder engine of the 911 Turbo delivered 260bhp, 300bhp from 1977 onwards with a 3.3-litre capacity. Top speed was over 160mph (257kph) and the zero to 60mph (96.5kph) time just a few fractions over five seconds.

For many, this car represented the pinnacle of 911 engineering, a supercar that could stand comparison with any Ferrari or Lamborghini. For Porsche, however, it represented the end of an era. In 1989, the factory confirmed that the Turbo had reached the end of the road. It was yesterday's car. Already, the Carreras 4 and 2 were defining the 911 standards for the 1990s. There would be a new Turbo, too – when the time was right. With the 959 as the ultimate evolutionary extension of the 911, it was clear that the career of the turbocharged flat-six was far from finished.

2 911: The Original Supercar

The difference between a sports car and a supercar is merely one of perception. By exploiting this disarmingly simple, if mildly heretical, idea Porsche has spanned the best part of three decades with a single model which, as the company likes to put it, expresses *driving in its purest form.*

Indeed, the 911 has made the transition from one to the other in the course of its twenty-seven years and quarter-million pro-duction run so gracefully and effortlessly, one can only conclude that Ferry Porsche's often-quoted tenet is truthful and more than mere inspiration. He holds that its concep-tion was a result not of natural competition or fashion pressure but rather 'a personal desire to create a car that would realise all the many joys of driving'. With the wisdom of hindsight, of course, it has done nothing more than better itself with each successive

This is where the family Porsche lived in 1935. The house, in Feuerbacher Weg, incorporates the garage where the first VW-based prototype was built.

Carrera RS 2.7. All were white, but some had blue wheels and side stripes, some red and some green. It doesn't do to be fussy now, though. These are much sought-after machines.

year — it's the ever-changing market that has altered its perceptions and classifications.

Love it or hate it — and there are flaws in this car no amount of development will ever erase — the 911 is a truly transcendental design that has evolved so smoothly and gradually that the only way to assimilate the changes is to jump a handful of years at a time. Because the 911 has remained a constant in an ever-changing automotive world, it has imposed a powerful 'intelligence' on the dubious principles that underpin the performance car market. Without obviously influencing its peers it has, by example, shown that two seats and a canvas top have nothing to do with performance, handling or seat-of-the-pants driving satisfaction.

As we all know today, many a plain Jane saloon or front-drive hatchback offers potent driving rewards — clearly not because they adhere to the classic front-engine rear drive formula but because they have been developed and engineered by people who know

about driving. Ferry Porsche wanted to drive a small car with light, informative steering yet with enough room for additional seats and a reasonable boot. It should be a car that was fast on the open road but docile in town. A car with superior traction to deal with the poorly-surfaced roads and steep hills of his native Austria. Given such a design brief, the wonder isn't that it turned out the way it did but that it offered such a scintillating driving experience from day one. For a car that, from a conventional point of view, was all wrong, it was all right.

It is that original single-mindedness and clarity of vision that has sired some of the great performance cars of three decades — from the frenetic 911S to the sensational 2.7-litre Carrera RS to the pulverisingly rapid 3.3 Turbo.

FUTURE SHOCK

No one would have put money on such a car ever being made back in 1947 when the

Lotus Elans provided keen competition on the track for 911s in the 1960s, making up for their relative lack of power with very nimble handling.

911S Targa with removable roof section. Targas are less popular with collectors because of the problems associated with the roof.

Cutaway for flat-six clearly shows the horizontally-opposed alignment of cylinders. Note the cooling fins around the cylinder barrels. The engine is very compact.

The 911 was sometimes used as a basis for styling exercises. This one, by Italian master Bertone, renders the familiar shape unrecognisable.

Porsche family decided to earn a living making their own cars (from old VW parts) instead of designing them for other people. Sixteen years later at the Frankfurt Motor Show, however, a picture of just how exciting the future might be was beginning to take shape as the 911 made its international debut, effectively replacing the 356.

Conceived as the 'Type 7' and originally to be named the 901 – until Peugeot objected to the use of 'their' three figure designation style with a zero in the middle – the 911's main selling points over its predecessor were greater refinement, a roomier cabin and boot, more performance and crisper handling. The extra urge, of course, was vital and provided, initially, by a 2-litre flat-six

engine slung, like the 356's flat-four, behind the rear axle line.

Drawings of the 'Type 7' date back to 1956 and, from these, Dr Porsche's eldest son, Ferdinand 'Butzi', designed the 911. His brief was to come up with a shape that would brand the new car an obvious descendant of the 356 while, at the same time, making it fresh enough to go several years without major modification. You only have to look at the latest Carrera 4 to appreciate the magnitude of his success.

Erwin Kommenda, the company's body engineer, made Butzi's drawings and models a production reality and four prototypes were built. One of these was a full four-seater but nothing came of it because Pors-

Early (2-litre, carburettor-fed) example of flat-six ready to be slotted into a car. This version developed 130bhp.

Ferry Porsche

Son of Professor Ferdinand Porsche, the man responsible for the design of the VW Beetle, Ferdinand Alexander Porsche II, 'Ferry', still holds the reins at Porsche, bending occasionally to the influence of his sister, Louise Piech.

With guidance from his father, Ferry saw the 356 into existence and conceived the 911. It was his desire that his eldest son, Butzi, should take over the family business but this led to a family rift and several younger members, including Ferdinand Piech, quit in 1972.

In the wake of the turbulence, Ferry Porsche hired Dr Ernst Fuhrmann as manager and gave him the unenviable task of finding a replacement for the 911. But, as recent history illustrates only too clearly, it wasn't to be that simple. Neither the 924 nor the 928 did anything to dim demand for the rear-engined Porsche, even though nothing was done to the 911 to sharpen its appeal.

A fundamental change of tack saw Fuhrmann replaced by Peter Schutz – his brief being to revive 911 development. But an initial climb in profits wasn't sustained. Schutz was out and accountant Heinz Branitzki in. It won't be for too long however, as he is nearing retirement. As I write, Ferry's youngest son, economist Wolfgang, thirty-seven, is waiting in the wings.

Porsche have always resisted change for change's sake, preferring instead to update and modify their cars only in small and carefully considered steps, often prompted by racing experience. The result of all these alterations is a car that's every bit as good judged by present standards as the original 911 was in its day. (Motor)

PORSCHE PROFILE

● The full title of Porsche, the company, is 'Dr Ing hcf Porsche AG'.

● 'AG' stands for 'Aktiengesellschaft' which, in German, means 'a joint stock company'. In Germany, a joint stock company is managed by an executive board and controlled by a board of directors. The Chief Executive at Porsche is Heinz Branitzki and the Chairman is Professor Dr Ing hcf Porsche.

● Porsche is the world's largest specialist manufacturer of high performance road cars.

● Porsche produced 32,183 cars in the financial year ending 31 July 1988.

● Total turnover in the 1987–1988 financial year was DM2,482 million (approx. £773m).

● On 31 July 1988, Porsche employed 8,218 people.

● Over twenty-five per cent of the workforce was employed at the research and development centre at Weissach.

● Forty per cent of all work now undertaken at Weissach is on behalf of other car makers, governments and even NATO. Actual turnover from research and development fees and licences, spare parts and repair work was DM397 million (approx. £124m) in 1987–1988.

● Porsche has won Le Mans twelve times – a record number of victories for a single car marque.

● In the UK, Porsche Cars Great Britain Limited is 100 per cent owned by Dr Ing hcf Porsche AG and has thirty-five official Porsche centres.

Cutaway of 911 Carrera shows that the engine sits well behind the rear axle line with transmission to the front of it.

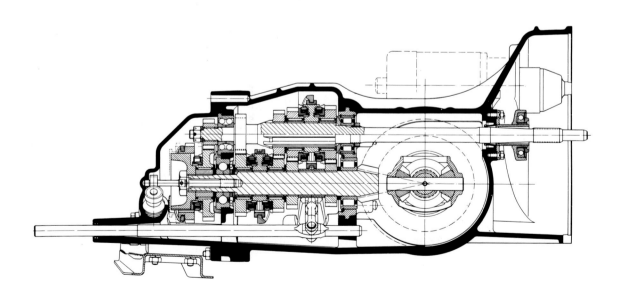

The 901/902 manual transmission was used in all 911 models up to 2.2 litres.

che didn't want to enter into direct competition with Daimler—Benz in the family car market.

PRACTICAL DECISIONS

Once this decision had been taken, a 2+2 chassis was developed for Butzi's body design. At this stage it was decided that the 911 would have no grease points, in keeping with a minimal maintenance policy.

With a decently dimensioned luggage area as a major priority, a very compact form of front suspension had to be devised. Longitudinal torsion bars attached to a

Porsche have managed to endow the car with so much pure feel, that we doubt that there is any car in the world which is as satisfying to drive hard. The steering is light, direct, responsive and has just the right amount of kickback — not so much that the wheel tugs strongly in your hands over bumps, but simply that it writhes gently, cementing a bond between your hands and the road surface . . .

. . . The 911's capacity to excite is perhaps for the wrong reasons. You could even argue that no car that sometimes takes over the driving process with such authority should be allowed on crowded roads. In truth, it's unlikely that most people will ever experience that side of the car's character, because Porsche's evolution process, not to mention the engineering wizardry, has pushed the wayward streak into the speed stratosphere. You're not likely to experience it more than once, anyway.
(Motor . . . Fast Lane)

chassis crossmember at the rear and to a lower wishbone pivot at the front provided the answer. Narrow MacPherson struts encased telescopic dampers but, without the conventional coil springs to intrude, made room for an ample boot at the front without ruining Butzi's low bonnet line. There was even sufficient space for a 62-litre (13.6-gallon) fuel tank under the floor of the boot.

As with the 356, torsion bars were used for rear springing, but its swing-axles were abandoned in favour of semi-trailing arms. While semi-trailing arms are viewed with some suspicion today, the margin of improvement they offered over swing axles is hard to overestimate.

A bigger car needed more power and while a version of the 1.5-litre flat-four Carrera engine designed by Dr Ernst Fuhrmann (later to become Porsche's Managing Director) might conceivably have sufficed in the short term, it was essentially a pure racing engine with roller bearings and twin camshafts on each bank. Although to some extent 'productionised' in 2-litre form with plain bearings, it wasn't really a cost-effective proposal for series manufacture.

The flat-six that was to become one of the most enduring production designs in automotive history was designed under the direction of Ing Hans Tomala. A six-cylinder configuration was chosen for smoothness and the initial capacity was 2 litres. Since the rear-slung location for the engine had already been decided, it was constructed from light alloys to minimise potential weight distribution problems.

Basic design parameters weren't hard to decide: air-cooling was an obvious requirement, as was a single overhead camshaft per cylinder bank. Toothed-belt drive was looked at in the interests of refinement but, after due consideration, ditched in favour of high quality Reynolds chains with an hydraulic tensioner for each bank.

But there was experimentation, too. Oil-cooled cylinders — another concession to refinement – were tried but didn't reach the required standard. The definitive prototype engine was code-named 821 which was virtually identical to the engine that went into production but with wet rather than dry sump lubrication. We mustn't forget Ferdinand Piech in all of this. He takes credit for the final design as head of engine development in 1964, and chief of development two years later.

SIX PACK

The Frankfurt Show launch caused quite a stir with the 911 being hailed as something of a packaging marvel, providing not only significantly more interior space than the 356 but fifty per cent greater glass area with its deeper windscreen and lower waistline. Amazingly, the 911 was 2.4in narrower than the 356 but the wheelbase was some 5in longer. With much less overhang, though, overall length was up by just 6in. The drag factor (Cd) of 0.381 bettered the 356's 0.40, too.

The final production design specification incorporated disc brakes all round and rack and pinion steering. In production form, the engine ran in eight bearings with a crankcase split vertically at the centreline of the forged steel crankshaft. The six pistons ran in individual finned barrels with chromed bores.

Something to celebrate. The 100,000th Porsche produced was a 911 Targa for the German police. They took delivery on 21 December 1966.

With an eye to the 911's track potential, dry sump lubrication was opted for. Over-square bore and stroke dimensions gave 80× 66mm and a swept capacity of 1,991cc with plenty of scope for future expansion. The outputs of this original engine were 130bhp at 6,100rpm and 128lb ft at 4,200rpm – impressive enough by the standards of the day but, with a 9.0:1 compression ratio and three triple-choke Solex 40 P1 carburettors, clearly leaving room for improvement.

An entirely new five-speed gearbox was designed for the 911 with Porsche-patented synchromesh on all ratios, a dog-leg first gate and drive taken to the rear wheels via fully articulated drive shafts. Painfully narrow – by today's standards – 165 tyres covered skinny 15×4½in (38×11.4mm) steel rims.

OUT OF TIME

Taking a look at the new 911's classmates back in 1964, it's genuinely hard to believe that they were the Porsche's contemporaries. Lotus was still a kit-car manufacturer and had just launched the Elan S2. The AC Cobra was in production but a long way from attaining classic status and Ferrari had won at Le Mans for the penultimate time. Most families were motoring around in Mark I Cortinas or, if they were well-heeled, Mark 10 Jaguars. Over in the USA, Ford was pulling the wraps off its very first Mustang and, in Italy, tractor-maker Ferrucio Lamborghini had only just built his first car. Where are they now?

True enough, some have come back as 'collectors cars' wearing house-style price tags, but does that make them any more essentially 'classic' than the perpetual Porsche? How many sports cars have improved enough to become the standard supercar reference?

It is interesting to note what Porsche sees as the major reasons for a level of customer

> *To many, the sound of a Porsche engine in full cry is music, a subtle mixture of muffled induction roar, fan whine and cam drive scream. At low speeds when you accelerate hard, some may consider the noise a mite obtrusive, though we feel that this is offset by the sound's unique quality.* (Motor)

loyalty that is the envy of most other car makers. It lists them thus: performance, reliability, residual value, quality and style. That's one way of quantifying the 911's enduring appeal. Another is expressed in *Motor* magazine's very first road test of the 911, re-printed here in full.

ROAD TEST

Reproduced from *Motor*

The 911 represents the second generation of production Porsches. The VW design ancestry, fast vanishing but still clearly recognizable in the previous 356 series, has disappeared without trace except that the 911 still has an air-cooled rear engine. But this engine is now a 2-litre flat-6 with inclined valves and overhead camshafts and it drives a close-ratio gearbox, with five speeds instead of four, which retains the delightfully smooth rapid action which made Porsche gearboxes famous; at the rear, swing axle suspension has been abandoned in favour of a low roll-centre design with trailing links and double-jointed drive shafts.

This clean sweep is equally apparent at the front; the trailing link Porsche front suspension, which became famous on pre-war racing Auto Unions and later ERAs has been replaced by a modified MacPherson layout with torsion bars instead of coil springs and steering is now by rack and pinion because this leaves the maximum room in the front luggage compartment. The whole car is roomier and the weight has increased by about 3 cwt.

In view of all this it comes as a surprise to find how much of a family resemblance remains. The seats, the low driving position, the black instruments calibrated with green markings, the subdued but beautifully finished interior, the layout, precision and smoothness of the controls are all characteristically Porsche. And so is the feeling of absolute solidity and freedom from minor rattles and creaks which you notice as soon as you drive away – the feeling that however bad the road surface you need never slow down out of consideration for the strength and durability of the car even though you may do so out of kindness of the occupants since some roads, particularly in France, generate a rather uncomfortable vertical bounce.

The subdued and pleasing noise from the back tells you where the engine is and so does the freedom from wheelspin and the ability to use a lot of the power on corners. But rear-engined handling characteristics have virtually disappeared – there are many front-engined cars which are more sensitive to crosswinds and very fast roll-free cornering can be enjoyed with no worries about losing the tail except in special circumstances. Performance figures show that the 911 is a very much faster car than its production predecessors; a maximum speed of 130mph on 130bhp says a lot for the drag coefficient and the acceleration times are astonishing for a 2-litre car weighing over a ton. It really comes into its own on long high speed journeys when the very smooth six cylinder power unit can be kept continuously in its best torque range between 3,000 and 6,000rpm by very free use of the superb, five-speed gearbox – this is no car for top gear drivers. Above all, it has that effortless feeling which suggests

that hard driving is what it is designed for and will never wear it out prematurely.

Performance and economy

Cars with one carburetter choke per cylinder hardly require rich mixture devices for cold starting and the Porsche doesn't have one at all. A few strokes on the throttle pedal to activate the accelerator pumps are all you need in sub-zero temperatures and although the idling is uncertain for the first mile or so, there is no hesitation or spitting back at all during the warming-up period. Hot starting, on the other hand, is poor – full throttle and a fair amount of churning away at the starter are usually necessary.

We spent many long periods virtually stationary in London traffic during the test and there was never any sign of hesitation or plug fouling. On the other hand, the engine doesn't like pulling hard below 1,500rpm and it only gets into its proper stride between 2,500 and 3,000rpm; after this it runs with complete smoothness and lack of strain to the rev limit of 6,800rpm. During the maximum speed runs the tachometer needle was sitting almost exactly on this limit at 130mph. It isn't a silent power unit – at low rpm there is a rumbling, rattling noise, which probably comes from the transmission, but once it rises into the useful torque range there is nothing but a smooth mechanical whirr and a hard, deep and very subdued exhaust roar which together form just the right accompaniment to fast motoring in a car of this purposeful character.

With a relatively low bottom gear and 60% of the unladen weight on independently sprung driving wheels, the Porsche accelerates from rest with remarkable rapidity – even when starting on the 1-in-3 test hill – reaching 50mph in 6.3 sec, 100mph in 24.3 sec; these are impressive figures for a sports car of any size let alone a 2-litre of particularly rugged construction.

In spite of air-cooling and a compression ratio of 9 to 1, Porsche claim that fuel of 96 octane rating is satisfactory and this was confirmed by our experience – there was no pinking on British or Continental premium grades. Long distance motoring in France and Italy at cruising speeds around 90mph showed a fuel consumption of about 21mpg and, with a 13½-gallon tank and a warning light to show when 1½ gallons remain, this meant that 250-mile stages were practicable between refuelling stops. English motoring, with its heavy town traffic and short sharp bursts of acceleration and braking proved much less economical (about 16mpg when trying hard) so that the overall figure fell to 19.2mpg.

Transmission

To appreciate a 911 you should be the sort of motorist who derives a positive pleasure from exercising a superb five-speed gearbox to maximum advantage. The synchromesh has that smooth, slicing action which is a Porsche speciality, the ratios are very close together and the gears are almost silent except, as mentioned before, at low speeds. To be always in the right gear for the present or potential situation demands little physical effort but a certain dedication and fore-thought which some will enjoy and others disdain. In winding and hilly country four of the five ratios may be used in constant succession.

The gear lever is arranged in such a way that the upper four ratios occupy the same positions as with an orthodox four-speed box; bottom gear is further left and back with reverse opposite and this plane is protected by strong lateral spring loading across the gate. Top gear is not an overdrive so this is a sensible and convenient layout; if you feel unhurried or lazy you can, in fact, treat it as a four-speed box and take off from rest in the 60mph second gear.

The clutch operation doesn't quite live up

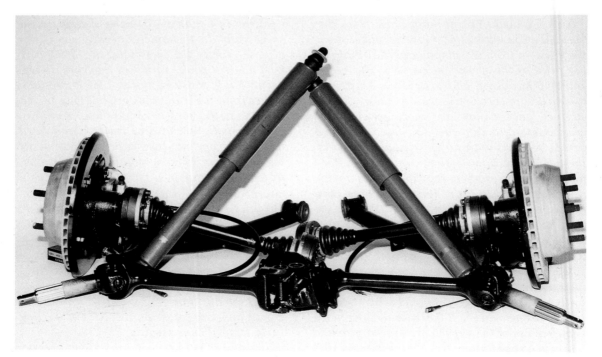

The 'bones' of 911's semi-trailing arm rear suspension.

Ventilated front disc brake and five-stud hub fixing.

to this standard. It is light but it has a long travel and an 'overcentre' feel – the pedal force rises to a maximum of 30lb. and then diminishes again as you press it further down. It may well be that careful adjustment would make a considerable improvement.

Handling and brakes

The 911 is the clearest refutation yet of the theory that rear-engined handling problems are insoluble without reverting to extreme counter measures which themselves have undesirable side effects. The basic oversteering influence of a 40/60 (unladen) weight distribution is counteracted largely by a very high roll stiffness at the front and a consid- erable difference between front and rear wheel camber settings; a large difference between front and rear tyre pressures is not called for.

In fact, one might almost criticise the handling on the grounds that it is too neutral – the car can be pushed up to its very high cornering speeds without a clear indication to the driver of what will happen when it finally lets go. On dry roads this doesn't matter very much – it is most stable accelerating round a corner, when it maintains a very mild understeer, but the limits are so high that few people will reach them on public roads. On slippery surfaces the German Dunlop SP high speed tyres still

Collapsible-type bumpers were fitted in 1973 but, prior to that, more conventional 'overrider' arrangements were used, as here.

grip tenaciously but the back end will break away if you use too much throttle in a low gear, or if you corner too fast on a trailing throttle – a moderate amount of power gives the best results. If you want to drive near the ragged edge you must remain alert because the usual early warning symptoms of roll, tyre squeal and attitude change are almost absent.

One of the very real advantages of a rear engine position is that it relieves the weight on the steering wheels; in this case they carry 8cwt. between them and it has therefore been possible to provide steering which is very high geared but also light. Possibly to prevent it feeling too light at high speeds, a high castor angle is used (7¾°) and in combina-

In general, early 911s made plentiful use of bright trim for detailing.

tion with large wheels and tyres and a reversible rack-and-pinion mechanism, this gives the steering a rather lively feel – camber changes, bumps, ridges, all feed back their messages quite strongly (but not harshly) to the driver's hands, particularly when cornering fast. Initially this gives a slightly disconcerting impression that external forces are trying to take charge – after a few hundred miles it isn't even noticed any more. The 911 was completely stable at its maximum speed on a smooth road.

An unusual feature of the all-disc braking system is that it uses a duo-servo drum handbrake – the drums are incorporated in the centre portion of the rear discs. This is

Performance

Conditions

Weather: Cold, dry, no wind.
Temperature: 40°–45°F. Barometer: 29.45 in Hg.
Surface: Dry tarmacadam.
Fuel: Premium grade, 98 octane (RM).

Maximum speeds

	mph
Mean of opposite directions (kilometre)	129.8
Best one-way kilo (5th gear)	130.2
4th gear	105
3rd gear	87
at 6,800 rpm	
2nd gear	60
1st gear	37

Acceleration times

mph	sec
0-30	2.8
0-40	4.4
0-50	6.3
0-60	8.3
0-70	11.0
0-80	13.7
0-90	18.5
0-100	24.3
0-110	31.8
Standing quarter mile	16.1

mph	5th gear sec	4th gear sec
10-30	–	–
20-40	11.4	8.0
30-50	9.0	7.1
40-60	9.5	6.8
50-70	8.9	6.2
60-80	8.1	7.5
70-90	9.5	8.0
80-100	10.2	10.5
90-110	11.8	–

Speedometer

Indicated	10	20	30	40	50	60	70
True	8½	19	29	38½	48	58	68

Indicated	80	90	100	110	120	130
True	77	86	95½	105	114	124

Distance recorder .... 2½% fast

Hill climbing

At steady speed		lb/ton
5th	1 in 7.4	(Tapley 300)
4th	1 in 5.5	(Tapley 400)
3rd	1 in 4.0	(Tapley 540)
2nd	1 in 2.8	(Tapley 745)

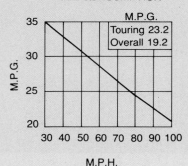

FUEL CONSUMPTION

M.P.G.
Touring 23.2
Overall 19.2

M.P.H.

Fuel consumption

Touring (consumption midway between 30 mph and maximum less 5% allowance for acceleration 23.2mpg
Overall 19.2mpg
(= 14.7 litres/100km)
Total test distance .... 2,800 miles
Tank capacity (maker's figure) 13.6gal

Brakes

Pedal pressure, deceleration and equivalent stopping distance from 30mph

lb	g	ft
25	0.20	150
50	0.65	46
75	0.96	31
100	0.98	30½
Handbrake	0.44	68

Fade test

20 stops at ½g deceleration at 1 min intervals from a speed midway between 30 mph and maximum speed (=80mph)

	lb
Pedal force at beginning	50
Pedal force at 10th stop	55
Pedal force at 20th stop	60

Steering

Turning circle between kerbs:	ft
Left	31½
Right	31¼
Turns of steering wheel from lock to lock	2¾
Steering wheel deflection for 50ft diameter circle	0.85 turns

Clutch

Free pedal movement .... =1¾in
Additional movement to disengage clutch completely .... =4¼in
Maximum pedal load .... =30lb

Weight

Kerb weight (unladen with fuel for approximately 50 miles) 20.4cwt
Front/rear distribution 40/60
Weight laden as tested 24.1cwt

Parkability

Gap needed to clear a 6ft wide obstruction parked in front 5ft 2in.

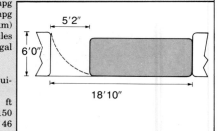

5'2"
6'0"
18'10"

very powerful — it held the car easily on a 1-in-3 hill and it recorded a most creditable 0.44g stop from 30mph. The discs are entirely adequate for a very fast car — the fade test gave a small rise in pedal pressure but no fade or roughness — they are light to operate and they showed very high stopping power on a dry road. They seem, however, to be biased in favour of dry conditions when weight transfer demands a high proportion of effort on the front. On slippery surfaces we experienced rather premature front wheel locking and it is certainly not advisable in this car to arrive too fast at sharp corners and try to negotiate them with the brakes still on.

Comfort and controls

The adjustable rake seats are rather firm and unyielding and nearly everyone who drove the car a short distance complained of aches and pains. Curiously enough, however, those who drove it a very long distance became more and more comfortable and after a couple of days acclimatization found that they could occupy them for 400 miles at a stretch without moving or fidgeting. Possibly the Porsche seat designers know best and the human frame needs time to adapt to the shape which suits it.

Considerably more side support would be an advantage in such a fast cornering car and for anyone of average height, or less, the driving position is too low, particularly in bad weather when the slightly raised instrument console is topped by a small unwiped arc of screen. In fact the accessory price list says that seats can be raised by 0.8in. for a cost of five guineas. The rather large steering wheel might also be moved a little further away or the gear lever a little nearer — a long-arm driving position tends to put the latter out of reach. Otherwise the driving position is excellent; the pedals are well-spaced and heel and toe operation of brake and accelerator is one of the easiest and most natural movements we have met in any car.

It is difficult to summarize the riding qualities of the Porsche. There is little road noise or harshness and, as we have remarked, a feeling of immense strength and solidity. On some well-known roads we were surprised by the ease and comfort with which it traversed indifferent surfaces at very high speed. Others aroused a rather rapid bouncing motion which was tiring and unpleasant and this characteristic was particularly noticeable in northern France. It may well be a penalty of the very firm damping which was appreciated when taking humps and dips at speed — the Porsche never seems to crash through to the limit of its spring travel as most cars do when hurrying over bad roads.

There is enough noise inside the car to remind you that this is a sporting machine but certainly not enough to be either annoying or tiring. Some wind roar is audible from about 80mph upwards but it increases comparatively little until the speed exceeds 100mph when the windows start to shudder slightly as interior pressure builds up — cutting off the fresh air and heater supplies postpones this condition and makes the car appreciably quieter.

Perhaps the biggest disadvantage of air-cooled engines is the difficulty of producing a first class heating system. Air is blown into the interior by the engine cooling fan and heated by passing round the exhaust manifolds. It can be discharged at foot level through vents with sliding gates or, by closing these vents, diverted to the windscreen nozzles for de-frosting. In addition there is a direct supply of cold fresh air from a submerged intake just forward of the windscreen controlled by a separate lever under the facia. The flow through this is not very large but it helps to avoid too much stuffiness at head level. The hot air supply fluctuates in temperature with engine output and needs frequent adjustment by means of a rather sensitive lever mounted on the floor just ahead of the gear lever; this lever is difficult to reach when safety belts are worn. We found that de-misting was not good in wet weather

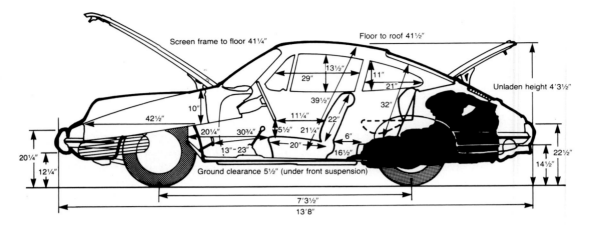

Screen frame to floor 41¼"

Floor to roof 41½"

Unladen height 4'3½"

13½"
29"
11"
21"
39½"
10"
32"
42½"
22"
11¼"
20¼" 30¾" 5½" 21¼"
6"
20"
13"-23"
16½"
20¼"
22½"
12¼"
14½"

Ground clearance 5½" (under front suspension)

7'3½"
13'8"

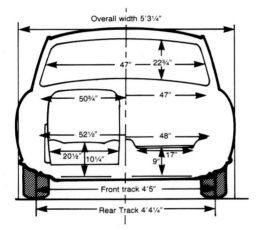

Overall width 5'3¼"

47" 22¾"
47"
50¾"
52½" 48"
17"
20½" 10¼" 9"

Front track 4'5"

Rear Track 4'4¼"

Ground clearance 5½" (under front suspension)
Scale 1:40 approx   7'3½"   13'8"
Bottom of door to ground 13"
Seat measurements taken with seats compressed
Height of male figure 5'10" approx
Height of female figure 5'4" approx

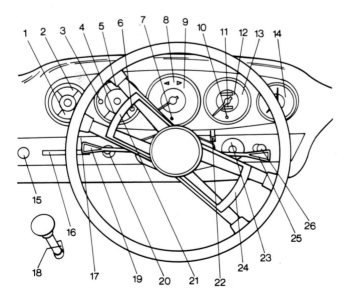

1 2 3 4 5 6 7 8 9 10 11 12 13 14
15
16
18 17 19 20 21 22
23
24
25
26

1 Low fuel warning light, 2 Fuel guage,
3 Generator warning light, 4 Handbrake
warning light, 5 Oil temperature guage, 6 Oil
pressure warning light, 7 High beam light,
8 Direction indicator light, 9 Tachometer,
10 Parking light indicator, 11 Trip recorder,
12 Total mileage recorder, 13 Speedometer,
14 Clock, 15 Radio, 16 Ashtray, 17 Fresh air
control, 18 Hot air control, 19 Windscreen
washer and wiper controls, 20 Cigarette
lighter, 21 Horn, 22 Trip re-set, 23 Ignition/
starter switch, 24 Horn, 25 Indicators/
dipswitch, 26 Main light switch

Specification

Engine

Cylinders .... Horizontally opposed flat 6
Bore and stroke .... 80mm × 66mm
Cubic capacity .... 1991 cc
Valves .. Inclined, operated by rockers from single ohc in each bank
Compression ratio 9:1
Carburettors ...... 2 Weber 40 IDA 3C triple choke
Fuel pump .... Bendix electric
Oil filter .... Fram or Purolator full flow
Max power (net) .... 130 bhp at 6,100 rpm
Max torque (net) .... 130lb ft at 4,300 rpm

Transmission

Clutch .... 8½in Fichtel and Sachs sdp
5th gear (s/m) 0.821
4th gear (s/m) 0.962
3rd gear (s/m) 1.216
2nd gear (s/m) 1.778
1st gear (s/m) 2.833
Reverse 3.147
Final drive ... 31/7 spiral bevel (ratio 4.428)
Mph at 1,000 rpm in:−
5th gear 19.4
4th gear 15.45
3rd gear 12.8
2nd gear 8.8
1st gear 5.45

Chassis

Construction .... Integral

Brakes

Type .... ATE discs all round with duo-servo drum-type handbrake incorporated in rear discs

Dimensions .... 11.1in front, 11.2in rear
Friction areas:
Front .... 16.2sq in of lining operating on 183sq in of disc
Rear .... 12.4sq in of lining operating on 177 sq in of disc

Suspension and steering

Front .... MacPherson type with damper struts, transverse lower wishbones, torsion bar springs and anti-roll bar
Rear .... Independent, by single trailing wishbones each side and transverse torsion bars
Shock absorbers:
Front and rear .... Boge telescopic
Steering gear .... ZF rack and pinion
Tyres .... Dunlop SP 165 HR-15
Rim size 4½J

Coachwork and equipment

Starting handle .... No
Jack .... Lever-type strut
Jacking points .. One each side under doors
Battery ...... 12-volt negative earth, 45amp hrs capacity
Number of electrical fuses 12
Indicators .... Self-cancelling flashers
Screen wipers .... 3-speed, self-parking
Screen washers .... Electric
Sun visors .... 2 (one with mirror)
Locks:
With ignition key ...... Both doors (and thus boot, engine room and fuel tank)
With other keys .... Glove box
Interior heater .... Standard. Air ducted from engine fan and heated by exhaust manifolds. Separate cold air intake at front

Extras .... Sun roof, chrome plated or magnesium alloy wheels, auxiliary lamps, safety belts, overriders, radio, leather upholstery, headrest, electrically heated rear window, roof rack etc.
Upholstery .... Leatherette
Floor covering ...... Reinforced nylon carpet
Alternative body styles .. Targa convertible (L.H.D. only)

Maintenance

Sump ...... 15¾ pints SAE 30HD (summer), 20HD (winter)
Transmission ...... 4¼ pints SAE 90 hypoid
Steering gear .... Not required
Cooling system .... Air-cooled
Chassis lubrication .... None
Minimum service interval ... 6,000 miles or twice a year
Ignition timing .... At TDC static
Contact breaker gap 0.016in
Sparking plug gap 0.014in
Sparking plug type .... Bosch W250 P21 (platinum electrodes)
Tappet clearances (cold) .... Inlet .004in Exhaust .004 in
Valve timing:
Inlet opens .... 29°btdc
Inlet closes .... 39°abdc
Exhaust opens .... 39°bbdc
Exhaust closes .... 19°atdc
Front wheel toe-in .... 15-20ft (approx ¹⁄₁₆in)
Camber angle .... 4°
Castor angle .... 7¾°
Kingpin inclination .... 10° 56ft
Tyre pressures .... Front 26lb, rear 29lb. (Plus 3lb all round for extended motorway driving)

Maintenance Summary

A. Engine

Every 3,000 miles − check valve clearances. Every 6,000 miles − change engine oil, renew oil filter, clean oil strainer and filter magnets. Check sparking plugs, cylinder compressions, distributor adjustments, ignition timing, fan belt tension and idling speed. Clean fuel pump strainers and change air cleaner element.

B. Transmission

Every 6,000 miles − change oil, check clutch pedal free travel.

C. Brakes

Every 6,000 miles − inspect for leaks and safety, remove pads, inspect and measure wear.

D. Suspension and steering

Every 6,000 miles − check tyre pressures and wheelbearing play.

E. Electrical

Every 6,000 miles − check functioning and battery condition.

and the cold air supply inadequate in warm climates in spite of built-in air extractor slots above the rear window. The rear quarter windows hinge outwards and so do the front ones which have particularly stiff and awkward catches.

On main beam the headlights are quite powerful – by contrast the dipped beam is rather disappointing and in misty weather it is noticeable that there is quite a lot of vertical scatter.

Fittings and furniture
One of the best features of the 911 is that it has windscreen wipers which are really effective. They have enough pressure to clear drying mud and they don't lift off the screen at high cruising speeds. Moreover, they have three different speeds and they are inter-coupled with the electric screen washer to work automatically when the latter is used. Both wipers and washers are controlled by the left hand steering column lever; the right hand lever looks after direction indicators and headlamp dipping and when driving at night in bad weather we found this whole arrangement exceptionally convenient – all the controls you need frequently are at your fingertips.

Most of the usual instruments are provided except that there is no oil pressure gauge and, of course, no water thermometer; an oil temperature gauge replaces the latter but it never seemed to move very far over the scale and certainly it never approached the recommended limit of 130°C. Black-faced dials with green calibration marks are not particularly easy to read although they show up well at night under facia lighting. Cigarette lighter, dimming mirror, an accurate clock and excellent reversing lights are all included as standard equipment.

The fuel filler flap and front luggage locker are opened by release knobs at the left hand end of the facia and access to the engine is controlled by a knob in the rear edge of the near side door frame; so when the car is

locked, all these are locked automatically. There are elastic pockets in each door, small map pockets just ahead of the doors and a lockable glove box in the facia; there is, of course, an enormous amount of stowage space behind the front seats when the back is unoccupied.

Servicing and accessibility
As there are no chassis greasing points at all, lubrication servicing is confined to changing engine and transmission oils at 6,000-mile intervals and cleaning or removing various filters. As the engine has dry sump lubrication, the dipstick (concealed beneath the oil filler cap) should only be read when the engine is running and the oil warm. The difference between low and high marks represents over 3½ pints and since we recorded an oil consumption of about 400 miles to the pint, this rather tedious job is not often necessary.

The rest of the service schedule, which involves quite a lot of work, is also based on 6,000-mile intervals with one exception – the handbook suggests that valve clearances should be checked every 3,000 miles. We doubt whether many owners have the time or the inclination either to do this themselves or to part with the car so frequently. Accessibility of engine components is generally very good and the battery, windscreen washer bottle, spare wheel, hydraulic reservoir and tools all live at the front where they are very easy to check. The jack is an ingenious column type operating on a friction grip principle; we found it a little difficult to master at first but remarkably quick and efficient in operation.

MAKE: Porsche. **MODEL**: 911. **MAKERS**: Porsche K.G., Postfach 85, Stuttgart-Zuffenhausen, W. Germany. **U.K. CONCESSIONAIRES**: Porsche Cars (Great Britain) Ltd., Falcon Works, London Road, Isleworth, Middlesex.

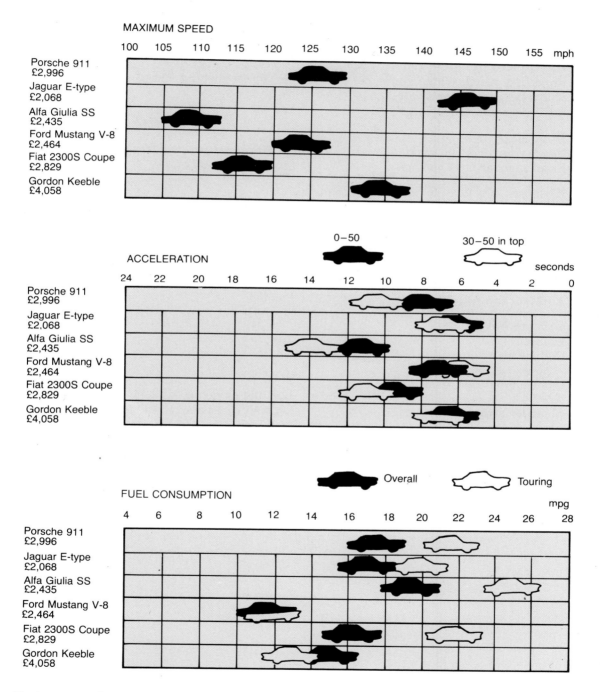

Maximum speed, acceleration and fuel consumption compared on some of the sports cars. The Porsche 911 is well up with the leaders on all counts.

Safety check list

1 Steering assembly	
Steering box position	Behind front wheel centre line
Steering column collapsible?	Yes, double jointed
Steering wheel boss padded?	Over small area
2 Instrument panel	
Projecting switches etc.?	Yes, mostly behind wheel
Sharp instrument cowls etc.?	No
Effective padding?	Yes
3 Door structure	
Interior handles and winders	Handles recessed, winders project
Front quarter-light catches	Projecting
4 Ejection	
Anti-burst door latches?	Yes
Child-proof locks?	No – only two doors
5 Windscreen	Laminated
6 Back of front seats	Padded
7 Windscreen pillars	Padded
8 Driving mirror	
Framed?	Yes
Collapsible?	No
9 Safety harness	
Type	Lap and diagonal, adjustable
Shoulder strap anchorages	On body sides above rear wheel arches
Floor anchorages	Well placed

3 The Legend Grows

Back in 1983 a Porsche Turbo competed in the 'World's Fastest Production Car' trial and blew the opposition away. Its victory came as less of a surprise to the Porsche camp than the Lamborghini and Aston Martin supporters, both of whom had until then assumed that the 911 Turbo was nothing more than a puffed-up pretender and that the blue steel, thoroughbred muscle of their champions – the Countach LP 500 and the V8 Vantage respectively – would naturally carry the day. It was a case of bulldog spirit versus Latin fire.

I confess to being as surprised as anyone. My job was to whip the Lamborghini's alleged 430 horsepower into a frenzy of superheated invincibility and devour the standing kilometre so rapidly that the others wouldn't see which way we went.

There was good cause to feel confident in this endeavour. I trusted the Countach and knew that it was a good one. The property of affable demolition consultant and sometime Thundersports racer Barry Robinson, 'BR 33' had already starred in a *Motor* road test and recorded the swiftest production car 0–60mph (0–96.5kph) time in the magazine's eighty-year history – a scintillating 4.8 seconds. By comparison, the 5.3 seconds for the 911 Turbo looked like the effort of a lame carthorse. The champagne was being chilled even as I fired up the Countach for the first run.

By the end of the third and final run, however, the bubbles had gone flat. The Porsche had proved quicker than the Lamborghini throughout and lifted the laurels with a best time of 23.985 seconds against the Italian car's best of 24.310 seconds. Perhaps what was even more telling, was that the Aston Martin was so far off the pace – a full second behind the Countach at 25.314 seconds – its mechanics were seen scratching their heads and wandering around in a daze.

SURPRISE PUNCH

Probably like the rest of us, they'd placed too much store by 0–60mph (0–96.5kph) times. On that basis, both the Aston and the Lamborghini had the Porsche well beaten. But this had been a contest over a set *distance* and one long enough to minimise the influence of short sprint prowess. The Porsche's tremendous traction off the line meant that it covered a lot of ground very quickly, its four-speed gearbox cut down time-wasting shifts and its relatively slippery shape ensured a sustained surge of acceleration all the way through to its 136mph (219kph) terminal speed at the kilometre post. Given that reasoning, it was always going to come first, though no one except the Porsche people could see it.

Then again, the 911 has always been an easy car to underestimate and a hard car to frame in its proper perspective. The legend has grown, as much as anything, out of the conflict between what its design suggests it ought to do and what it actually does. And this is also the reason for its enduring fascination with the motoring press.

CONFLICTING REPORTS

Not even *Motor* could have anticipated the controversial issue that the 911's handling was to become over the ensuing decades with opposing camps of media protagonists arguing the toss with barely disguised passion. The handling was either extremely tricky and dangerous or merely a challenge to be overcome by a degree of sensitivity and understanding at the helm.

By the time I came to write my first 911 road test I reckoned I'd made up my mind. The year was 1983 and the model a 3-litre SC Cabriolet. The 911's handling had by then, of course, become much more 'forgiving', but it's interesting to compare what

I wrote in 1983 with *Motor's* original findings some sixteen years earlier. And bear in mind that when I wrote the test, I'd never set eyes on the latter . . .

'The extent to which Porsche have turned chassis theory on its head with the latest 911s remains one of modern motoring's most notable achievements. Sixty-one per cent of the Cabriolet's total weight is over the rear wheels which, in turn, are prone to undesirable camber changes under load due to their semi-trailing arm suspension. It should not add up, and yet the cabriolet bears witness to a triumph of development over design – up to a point, at any rate.

Original 911 Turbo: the wide body hurt the top speed but acceleration was spectacular, as was traction from gumball rear tyres.

Clues to Turbo cabin are few, though extra supportive seats and more extensive use of leather are the most obvious giveaways.

'Given the right conditions – a fast, open series of curves with a dry and not too bumpy surface – the Cabriolet is nothing short of sensational. Its sheer speed, compact dimensions and ease of all-round vision make a powerful contribution to its swiftness. The penny-clipping precision and writhing feedback of the steering, the unrelenting purchase of the fat (Pirelli) P7s on the tarmac and their unerring traction out of junctions and tight hairpins – it all makes the 911 almost paralysingly rapid across the ground and a driving experience of unmatched satisfaction.

In such circumstances, even the car's inherent tendency to oversteer if the throttle is shut mid-bend can be used to tighten a wide line should a corner be entered too fast: the resulting change in attitude is certainly abrupt but, by relaxing your grip on the steering wheel, steering castor action alone invariably applies just the right amount of corrective lock.

'Roads which are characterised by more demanding bumps, dips and crests, however, soon begin to pick holes in the Porsche's handling, promoting a sometimes worrying lack of

Supercars all, but which is the fastest? It isn't Italian.

911 Turbo with something to prove. And it did – beating off all comers over the standing kilometre to become the world's fastest-accelerating production car.

Aston Martin V8 Vantage looked spectacular but couldn't get close to the Porsche.

The author gives it some in the Countach. But it's not enough, the outlandish Lamborghini coming second to the 911.

stability and disconcerting front-end lightness. The car can be driven quicker than most, but the driver needs to have his wits about him. It is in the wet, however, that the Cabriolet demands most respect. Here, even the most skilled and experienced 911 driver can find himself in a dangerous 'Catch 22' situation: if he enters a greasy bend even a shade too fast the result can be massive understeer with the lightly-laden front wheels ploughing straight on, yet if he lifts off the tail will move out in a pendulous sweep that, unless extremely quick and positive steering action is taken, will spin the car. That is the extreme condition, but it is one the 911 driver does well to remember.'

LARGER THAN LIFE

So that's the nuts and bolts of the 911's dynamic identity: some good, some bad and a fascination out of all proportion to either. And it's that fascination that takes some explaining. Many have tried. This is *Car* magazine in January 1988, having just picked the 911 Carrera as one of their top ten cars: 'Those who love the 911, who believe that they can reach into its soul and understand it thoroughly, revel in the car's unforgiving behaviour, knowing that the rewards for correct technique are the greater for not being easily won. And what's more fundamental, they also know that the mounting of the engine outside its wheelbase confers large advantages on the car which simply would not otherwise be available.'

I had my say on the subject in my book *Supercars: the Myth and the Magic* and found it hard to be quite as positive:

'It is impossible to define *supercar* without thinking of the perpetual Pors-

che; the car, the strands of ability it weaves in the fabric of the breed, both black and white. I've talked to good drivers who would rather walk than drive a 911: the old-fashioned cabin annoys, the clonky gearchange irritates, the wayward on-the-limit handling caused by having the engine in the boot frightens. I know others who are loathe to drive anything else, relishing the very challenge it poses, slaves to the sounds and actions of that charismatic flat-six – and to its awesome performance if turbocharged – spoiled by the superb build quality and relative practicality . . .

'. . . For my part, I'm a hopeless fan of the engine, though I'm sure I couldn't live with the rest of the car. It's not one that suffers bouts of laziness. Always in the mood for serious motoring, there's little that could be mistaken for compromise in its character if you're not. The gearchange, for example, requires as much concentration to work smoothly in traffic as it does when you're blasting down a Welsh valley, low-flying Tornado filling the rear-view mirror. The pedals unnaturally sprout up from the toeboard like disfigured mushrooms, the switchgear is exquisitely haphazard, and important sections of the instrumentation are obscured by the steering wheel.

'The Porsche's big problem is that it never lets you forget about its shortcomings; you can only enjoy the *driving* once the machine has been mastered. By the standards of most modern fast cars, that's a perverse challenge.'

SPEEDSTER

George Kacher, *Car*'s German correspondent, has never pulled his punches when it comes to the 911 he is as responsible as anyone for de-mystifying its appeal. Writing in the December 1987 edition, he had this to say about the newly launched 911 Speedster:

'The latest 911 embodies all the vices and virtues its stablemates have become notorious for. It has a powerful engine which sounds better than my favourite CD. It has a surprisingly rigid chassis and a race-proven suspension which offers plenty of grip. And it is built to last with quality and durability designed into every single component. But the Speedster is by no means flawless. Take, for instance, the heavy clutch, the vague and rather slow gearbox, or the very unassisted steering which is neither well-balanced nor well enough damped. Look at the poor ergonomics, the bad ventilation, or the speed-sensitive heating. And consider the unsatisfactory directional stability, the car's susceptibility to crosswinds and the tricky handling in the tightrope demarcation zone between *wow!* and *ohmigawd!*

'Fact is though that, as with all 911s, the fascination will eventually outweigh the flaws. The 911 is a challenging car, and although there are now plenty of rivals which offer better handling, better roadholding, more comfort or even more power, it is this challenge of mastering the rear-engined monster which makes you come back time after time.'

SOMETHING TO PROVE

Ah, the rivals. More than any other 'super-car' the 911 has seen them come and go. The fact that it has outlived all the original pretenders to its crown and continues to see off most, if not all, newcomers perhaps says more about its timeless character than a formal explanation ever can. What were those original rivals? Mike McCarthy explained in *Classic and Sportscar* magazine in June, 1985:

'By the time the 911 was properly established, the car's most direct rival was probably the Jensen C-V8. The C-V8 was around £200 more expensive than the top of the line 911S and was substantially quicker to 60mph, managing the figure in 6.7secs compared to the Porsche's 8.0secs. But at the top end the Porsche won hands down at 137mph to the Jensen's 129mph.

'The Mercedes–Benz 230SL may have won over some potential Porsche customers, but purely on "chic" appeal. Similarly, Lancia's Farina Coupes and GT3C would qualify on an aesthetics and glamour basis, but would have lost out badly on the performance front at 911S money.

'By 1968 the choice was wider for the enthusiast, with between £3,228 (911T) and £4,385 (911S) to spend. At the cheaper end of the scale the pretty BMW 2000CS was a weak challenge with far inferior performance. The Lancia Flaminia suffered similarly.

'If only the Fiat Dino 2.4 Coupe had been properly marketed in right-hand drive form it may have made an appreciable impression on the Porsche market at similar money to the mid-range 911s. It cost £3,737 when Porsches ranged from £3,228 to £4,385. Top speed was around 130mph and 60mph could be reached in 8.5secs.

'The Jaguar E-type fixed-head coupe, by this time in 4.2-litre form, was a true competitor in all respects but price – you could buy nearly two for the price of a 911S. But the "E" wasn't quite as quick as the 2.4-litre Porsches.

The evolving 911 shape has sprouted spoilers, 'stylised' bumpers and numerous cosmetic details. . . .

. . . but nothing has corrupted the shape's basic appeal.

Ferrari 'Dino' 246GT and Jaguar E-type were 911
contemporaries. Both have gone on to become valuable classics.
911, however, is one classic that's still in production.

Early 911 Turbos quickly gained a reputation for being tricky to handle in all but the most experienced hands.

911 Cabriolet – a long time on the drawing board but worth the wait. The hood is excellent.

Carrera Club Sport – as quick to 60mph as a 3.3 Turbo, but with a crisper throttle response.

A very exclusive 911, indeed: the Turbo SE Cabriolet – more power and equipment than a regular Turbo plus a hugely inflated price tag.

Porsche's colour-coordination hasn't always been the best....

... black and tan is an acquired taste.

911 interiors are generally hard wearing. This one belongs to a 1977 3-litre Carrera.

Engine from the same car is showing its age but is mechanically sound.

1984 911 Carrera Targa came with 'phone dial' style alloy wheels.

'For the less sporting, the Jensen Interceptor and Mercedes–Benz 280SL may have tempted, both costing much the same as the 911S. The Aston Martin DB6 was also similarly priced and offered, at least in Vantage form, arguably superior performance.

'Perhaps the man who would have had to stretch himself financially even to afford the base 911T might have been persuaded to settle for the lovely Fiat 2300S – you could, after all, get those Abarth tuning bits for them. But the 2300, like the 130 Coupe that followed it, was not successful in this country. Neither was it nearly quick enough to compete with the contemporary Porsches.

'Renault–Alpine have always produced cars which might threaten Porsche, but the Dieppe-based company has never distributed its products this side of the channel. This also rules out the Ligier JS2 and Lancia Stratos. All these machines were very much homologation specials, making little pretence at being comfortable cars.

'The early seventies saw competition of a refined sort from Citroen with the SM and from Alfa Romeo with the bizarre Montreal. Other likely alternatives were the Mercedes–Benz 280SL, BMW 2800 coupe and the underestimated ISO Rivolta GT.

'With the introduction of the 2.7-litre Carreras, Porsche launched themselves into the supercar bracket. By 1973 the basic 911 cost £4,562 and the top of the range Carrera Touring £7,193. Discounting cars like the AC 428 (£6,914), Jensen Interceptor III (£6,981) and Mercedes–Benz 350SL

A superb example of the 911E. This is a 1974 example with targa top.

(Above): *911 Speedster recalled its 1950s namesake. It is seen here lapping the Nurburgring.*

(Left): *911 Cabriolet minus rear wing and looking the better for it.*

(£5,725), the classic comparisons came from Italy in the form of the Ferrari 246 Dino (£5,915), De Tomaso Pantera (£6,596) and Pantera GTS (£7,627), Lamborghini Uracco (£6,545) and from Germany with the BMW 3.0CSL (£6,899).'

THE FERRARI FACTOR

It is Italy and, to be more specific, Ferrari that has always given the 911 its stiffest opposition. First with the Dino, then the 308 which became the 328 and, latterly, the 'mini-Testarossa' 348. Back in 1985, *Fast Lane* pitted a Ferrari 308 GTS against a 911 Carrera Cabriolet and reached a controversial conclusion:

'Porsche's great achievement with the 911 has been to disguise its intentions, though not to eradicate them. It is still a difficult proposition when taken to its very high cornering limits; in our opin-ion it is at its most pleasant on the relatively modest tyre sizes supplied as standard (as tested here: 185/70 front and 215/60 rear, Dunlop D4s in this case, on 15in rims, 6J and 7J respec-tively) than on any of the wider, lower profile combination that are available for extra money.

'It is the way a Porsche 911 does things that makes it so appealing. There is plenty of feel from the steering and chassis, and you know well in ad-vance what it is about to do. If you cannot solve the problems it sets you, it is unfair to blame the car.

'The Ferrari will allow you to make a small error of judgement, and will let you step back from the brink, so long as you don't behave in a suicidal man-ner. The 911 has a will of its own, and you have to drive within the limits it sets. It simply isn't worth tempting fate in a downhill bend on a greasy surface; the result will be a desire to lock up the front wheels under braking, followed

PORSCHE 911S 2.4

Engine	Horizontally opposed 'six'
Capacity	2,341cc
Bore	84mm
Stroke	70.4mm
Valves	Sohc per bank
Compression	8.5:1
Max power	190bhp/6,500rpm
Max torque	159lb ft/5,200rpm
Transmission	5-speed, manual
Final drive	4.43:1
Brakes	Servo-assisted discs all round
Suspension	
Front	Independent by wishbones and torsion bars
Rear	Independent by semi-trailing arms and transverse torsion bars
Steering	Rack and pinion
Tyres	185/70VR15
Performance	
Max speed	144mph
0–60mph	6.1secs
Standing ¼ mile	13.9secs
Overall mpg	18.0

by strong understeer, and then almighty oversteer on lift-off. These tendencies are held much more in check than once was the case, but they are still there, lurking, waiting to catch out the unsuspecting or imprudent.

'That said, a well-driven Porsche, with its superb traction and tractability, will not be left behind its rivals on a twisty road. It is simply that the car reminds the driver of his mortality in a more fundamental manner than a Ferrari; like a 'tame' leopard it invites no one to take liberties. Its ride quality is noisy and firm (firmer than the 308's) but never actually harsh . . .

'. . . In terms of build quality, it is widely recognised that only another Stuttgart company stands above Porsche. All the panel fits on a 911 are immaculate, everything in the interior is excellent (apart from the door pulls, made of nasty plastic), and the paint finish is immaculate; Porsche cannot afford to be complacent, however – Ferrari has made great strides in all these areas in recent years . . .

'. . . If you want first-time-every-time starting and no messing about, the Porsche still holds sway over the Ferrari. Yet the 911 is more brutish than the 308, which is perhaps the most refined sporting car, in handling terms, in production today. It is as rewarding to drive as the German car without placing the driver on the knife-edge so often. As a *second* car it possibly makes more sense. . .

. . . By a majority vote *Fast Lane*'s team would choose the Ferrari, mainly on emotional grounds (such as the fact that it's one of the most beautiful cars in the world). If it came to the point where we had to write out cheques, on the other hand, the choice might be different.'

4 Carrera!

A 911 Carrera – any 911 Carrera – is special. 'Carrera' is the Spanish word for 'race' and, even by 911 standards, the models that wear the badge have something extra – that Nurburgring-at-dawn sense of occasion whenever they take to the road. Porsche pragmatists may never have regarded the marriage of sharpened knife-edge throttle response, less sound-deadening, a louder paint job and a harder ride as something to relish but, in practice, the removal of a little cotton wool was seldom a great loss. On the contrary, it had a number of clear-cut advantages.

The 3-litre Carrera RSR was perhaps the most outrageously purposeful of all the 'homologation special' 911s to take to the track. Its chillingly aggressive exhaust note sent shockwaves through slack-jawed spectators. Small boys' ice creams plopped on to their shoes – not so much at the sighting of the race-ready RSR but that the malevolent, hollow-throated howl should be coming from a 911.

The RSR was no ordinary 911. Despite the mechanical headaches involved in wringing just a little more steam out of the 3-litre flat-six that powered the RS, the result was, perhaps, the purest and most intense expression of the normally-aspirated 911. In building the RSR for the 1974 customer-racing season, the specific problem facing Porsche's engineers was with the engine's ever-thinner cylinder walls. The expedient solution was to add weight and rigidity by changing from magnesium to pure alloy for the die-cast crankcase and adopt 95mm Nikasil-coated bore dimensions necessary (with the 70.4mm stroke) to make the 3-litre capacity.

Because the 3-litre RS was an 'evolution' of the 2.7 version, Group 3 rules required that only 100 be built. In the event, Porsche produced 109 – forty-nine RSRs for racing and rallying and the rest in road-going trim. For many, the RS and especially the 330bhp RSR will forever remain the ultimate Carrera and, by definition, the ultimate 911 though since it is generally Porsche policy that the 'Carrera' name is granted to the fastest and the best, it's no surprise that the Carrera 4 and 2 currently represent the pinnacle of 911 engineering this side of the 959.

RS SETS THE PACE

The first 911 Carrera to make a big impact, however, was launched in 1972. Based on the 911S bodyshell, it was built in limited numbers for homologation purposes. By increasing the bore dimension of the flat-six from 84 to 90mm but retaining the same 70.4mm stroke, capacity was enlarged to 2,687cc and power raised to 210bhp at 6,300rpm. Tipping the scales at a lean 1,984.5lb (900kg), this was the RS and its performance caused a sensation with a top speed comfortably in excess of 150mph (241kph) and 0–60mph (0–96.5kph) acceleration in the mid-five second region.

This Carrera's *raison d'être*, of course, was competition and, initially, 500 were built for homologation into the Group 4 'Special GT' category. But this was just for starters. In fact, a total of 1,600 Carreras were built, thus widening its field of activity into Group 3. Some 600 of these had 911S-style trim and equipment, the rest were racers. The Car-

Perhaps the most extravagant production 911 of all, the Turbo SE Cabriolet offered unparalleled open air thrills.

rera's reputation and exclusivity were assured in Britain: just 100 of the road-going versions were imported in 1973.

Reaping extra power and torque through greater capacity was beginning to be problematical. With the regular engine, a bore of 87.5mm was the critical dimension: anything more and the block started to lose strength and rigidity. For the Carrera, therefore, the Biral cylinder inserts were ditched altogether in favour of the nickel-silicon carbide, Nikasil which Porsche's engineers used to coat the aluminium cylinder walls. The coating was just a fraction of a millimetre deep but extremely tough and not only eliminated wear but found a little more power by significantly reducing friction.

In other respects, the bigger capacity Car-

rera engine closely mirrored that of the 911S. The cylinder heads, for example, were identical. Yet outputs showed an encouraging climb – around ten per cent more power and an eighteen per cent increase in torque. A stronger clutch spring was in order. With the rev-limit increased to 7,300rpm and a distinct 'on-cam' surge of energy at around 4,000rpm, the RS piled thrills on top of the already exhilarating 911 driving experience and created a magic which has never waned (*see* Chapter 8).

WHITE HEAT

Aesthetically, the Carrera made a confident statement about its intentions. The initial batch used a livery of white with 'Carrera'

Carrera RSR was a popular and successful circuit car in the mid-70s.

Porsche 1977 SC.

emblazoned down the sides in blue or red; whichever colour was chosen was also picked out on the wheel centres. Just as distinctive was the 'duck tail' rear aerofoil formed out of the glass-fibre engine cover. Not only did this render the Carrera instantly recognisable but reduced rear-end lift from 320 to 93lbs at maximum speed and pushed the car more firmly on to the tarmac in fast sweeps. By moving the centre of air pressure back by 6in (15cm), it also made the car less sensitive to cross-winds.

The Carrera's appealing broad-shouldered look was mostly the result of the flared arches needed to accommodate the wider (7in (18cm)) rear rims – those at the front remained 6in (15cm). Suspension changes incorporated beefier anti-roll bars (18mm) and stiffer Bilstein dampers.

Despite the obvious similarities, the RS was really quite different to the 911S – so much so that it had to be built on a separate production line. For a start, no one was required to apply sound-proofing materials or undercoating – there wasn't any. Nor was any form of carpeting required; rubber mats were used instead. No rear seats, either, and those in the front were simplified to reduce weight. Further pounds were pared from the all-up weight by leaving off the glove-box lid, the standard door trim and even the coat-hooks. Since these last items couldn't have weighed more than a few ounces apiece, one is tempted to surmise that their exclusion was as much psychological as practical.

Even so, the weight loss was impressive. With a meagre 1,984lb (900kg) to haul around, it's little wonder the RS was rapid – and not just in a straight line. Tests revealed that with its lighter weight and fatter tyres it could corner with a lateral acceleration of 0.912g which equated to as much grip as any road-going 911 had ever had.

911 Turbo SE Cabriolet – SE stands for Special Equipment.

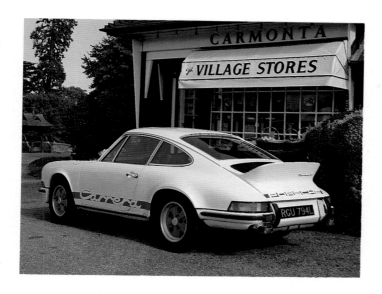

(Above and right): *Optimum 911 – the RS 2.7. Note the distinctive 'duck-tail' rear spoiler.*

(Below): *The spoiler didn't just provide downforce to push the car down on to the road, but supplied cooling for the engine, too.*

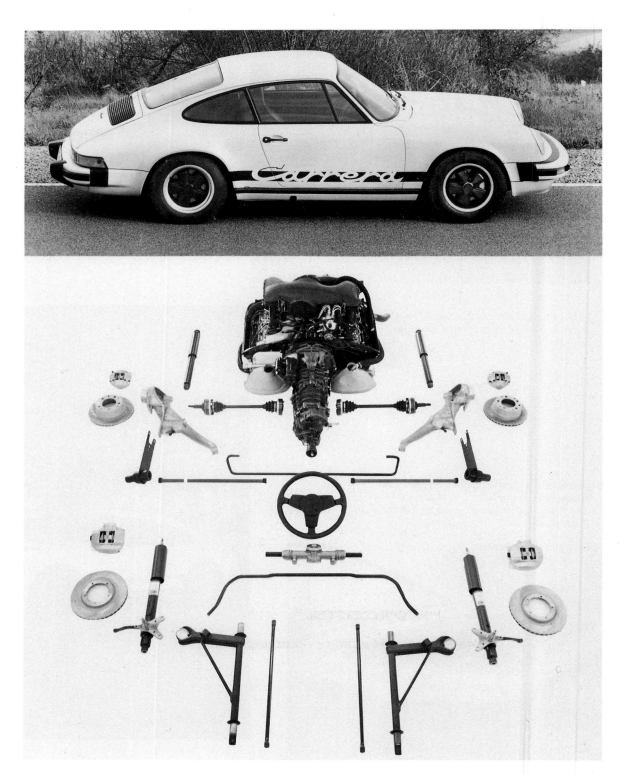

Carrera 2.7.

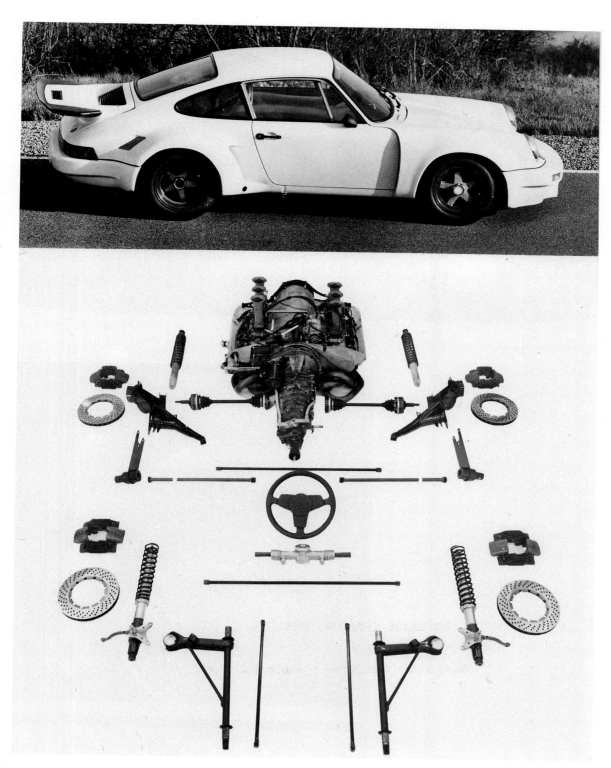

Carrera RSR 3.0.

2.7-litre engine developed 210bhp.

*The spare wheel in the front helped
even-out weight distribution.*

*Turbo SE's flat nose aped 935 racer's. Engine developed an extra
20bhp over 3.3's 300bhp.*

*Turbo SE's flat nose aped 935 racer's. Engine developed an extra
30bhp over 3.3's 300bhp.*

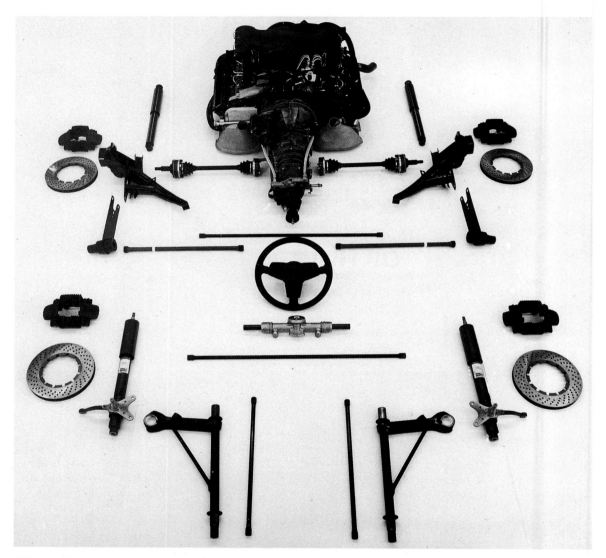

What makes a Carrera RS 3.0 tick.

So that was the birth of the Carrera and, in RSR form, the fruit of all the painstaking development was harvested. The RSR cleaned the board at three international and seven national championships and, at the height of its success, took both the Trans–Am and IMSA GT championships in America and also gained outright victory in the 1973 Targa Florio.

UNTIMELY TERMINATION

Carrera production continued in 1974, but the car was softened-up for series production. It was still based around the 2.7-litre engine with mechanical fuel injection – a combination which produced a stirring 210bhp – but all the 'weight saving' luxury

1975 Porsche 911 3-litre Turbo.

items had been put back. This wasn't the 'fat' Carrera, but there was no denying that it was a fleshier customer than the muscle-hard original. Out with the 'RS' appellation went the duck-tail rear spoiler for most markets though, in Britain, it was kept until 1975.

In America, however, the Carrera's days were numbered. For the 1974 model year (G-series), 2.7-litre 911s got Bosch K-Jetronic electronic fuel injection. The mechanical injection system of the Carrera failed to meet the increasingly tough American emission regulations and the model was subsequently withdrawn from that market.

A couple of years later, the 'Carrera' name disappeared altogether as part of a swinging 911 rationalisation. The Carrera (by now 3-litre) and 911 2.7-litre were dropped

to make way for a single model, the 911SC. This was, indeed, a year of momentous change for Porsche: the 911 Turbo went up in capacity to 3.3 litres, production of the front-engined 924 had hit its stride and 924's big brother, the 4.5-litre V8-engined 928, was poised for production.

In effect, the 911SC was a continuation of the Carrera and retained its basic specification, even down to the wide wheels and flared arches. Power came down from 200 to 180bhp, but a new cam profile resulted in a flatter torque curve and better engine flexibility.

The development that saw the return of the 'Carrera' name was as fitting as it was timely. In 1984, the Weissach technicians announced a version of the enduring flat-six that was 'eighty per cent new'. The all-alloy

911 Club Sport uses old RS's basic colour scheme.

Porsche 911 Turbo.

engine block retained the 95mm bore but, by using the Turbo's crankshaft, the stroke was increased to 74.4mm and, with it, the swept volume to 3,164cc. Maximum power leapt from 204 to 231bhp at the same engine speed (5,900rpm). Torque output received a similar boost, rising from 180lb ft at 4,200rpm to 209lb ft at 4,800rpm. Compression ratio was up, too – From 9.8 to 10.3:1 – under the influence of new pistons with higher domes. What a comeback. Not only did the new Carrera offer virtually Turbo pace but also better economy.

FASTER, FITTER

I have good cause to remember the first attribute. Not only was I present at the Millbrook testing ground on the day *Motor* achieved a top speed of 152mph (244kph) and 0–60mph (0–96.5kph) in 5.3sec from the Carrera, but I was driving the car on the evening it was stopped by the police for not

just breaking the speed limit but not having dropping within it for seventeen miles. All that and it still returned an overall consumption of 21mpg, exactly the same figure as that returned by the original 2-litre 911 tested by *Motor* back in 1965.

Part of the credit for the improved efficiency must go to the Bosch DME (Digital Motor Electronics) injection/management system which replaced the K-Jetronic and, like Motronic, mapped both injection and ignition requirements while juggling with variables such as throttle opening, engine temperature, engine loading and speed and so on. DME's other big contribution to fuel-efficiency was a petrol cut-off on the overrun. The inlet manifold was new and so too was the exhaust system.

Braking and transmission were other areas that received attention. Disc thickness was increased by 3.5mm and a pressure limiting valve (from the 928, as it happened) was fitted to reduce the 911's propensity to lock-up its lightly laden front wheels under

1978 911SC 3.0.

heavy braking on wet roads. A bigger (8in (20cm)) servo from the Turbo replaced the previous 7in (18cm) unit.

As for the gearbox, and oil cooler (type 915/67) was fitted and fourth and fifth gears lengthened to make the most of the extra power. The 3.2-litre 'six' was certainly an engine of character. It idled smoothly and pulled without hesitation from as little as 700 revs. Smaller, more highly-stressed Italian units were seldom as tractable. On the debit side, it wasn't all that exciting to listen to – not by Carrera standards, anyhow. At high revs it sounded a trifle muted and anodyne, lacking the scalp-tingling savagery of the 2.7-litre RS. At low-to-medium revs, though, it growled purposefully and delivered a mighty punch: in addition to a top speed of 152mph (244kph) and 0–60mph (0–96.5kph) in 5.2sec, the *Motor* magazine

road test of 1983 also recorded a 0–100mph (0–160kph) time of 13.6sec which was quite exceptional.

THE PRACTICAL SUPERCAR

The 911 Carrera's brakes – huge ventilated discs all round – were, like the rest of the chassis, an easy match for the performance, though the ride, while closely controlled at speed, could sometimes seem choppy around town. The seats were rather hard, too, but they went back far enough to cope with tall drivers and the 'boot' was big enough for several squashy bags. Instrumentation and switchgear, while comprehensive, were all too typical in their haphazard presentation. Visibility, however, has always been fairly

911 CARRERA CLUB SPORT vs 944 TURBO SE	911	944
cc	3,164	2,479
Max bhp	231	250
Max lb ft	210	258
Max mph	151	152
0–60 secs	5.2	5.7
30–70 secs	5.2	5.0
¼ mile	13.9	14.2
30–50 secs	5.4	7.4
50–70 secs	7.7	7.6
Overall mpg	20.6	19.1
Touring mpg	25.1	29.1
Mph/1,000rpm	24.3	25.3
Weight lb	2,608	2,699

good by supercar standards, though a rearward blind spot was created by the huge tail spoiler if specified.

The Carrera handled well. Even by the standards of its mid-engined peers, it was easy to be surprised by the speeds at which it was possible to take corners. These high cornering speeds followed as much from the immediate response and lack of roll as from the sheer cornering power – though this was so high that it was seldom exceeded on public roads in the dry.

The handling displayed the mild tendency for understeer common to all 911s. Once settled on its line, however, the power could be fed in at will, the driver secure in the knowledge that, in the dry at least, those fat rear tyres would need severe provocation to relinquish their purchase on the tarmac. With the road stretching out towards the horizon, the temptation to push the 911 Carrera hard was overwhelming. It remains one of the most rewarding of Porsches, the 'Rambo' of 911s.

5 Born to Race

The 911 made its motorsport debut in the 1965 Monte Carlo Rally, just two years after production started. Homologated in the Grand Touring class, power from the 2-litre flat-six was tweaked up from 130 to 160bhp, the gearing lowered, a limited-slip differential fitted, beefier rear brake calipers employed and the fuel tank stretched to hold 100 litres (22 gallons).

Hardly a transformation, but rallying had much firmer roots in reality back then and the 911, with its fine traction and on-demand oversteer, was good enough to give driver-engineers Herbert Linge and Peter Falk victory in the GT class and a promising fifth place overall.

It was promising indeed. The 911 never looked back on its way to becoming one of motorsport's outstanding success stories, a glittering career that peaked with a 700bhp 935 gaining outright victory at Le Mans.

The early successes, however, were all in rallying. In 1966, German driver Gunther Klass took a similarly prepared 911 to outright victory in the German Rally and ended the season as European GT Rally Champion. Mid-way through the year, the factory announced the 911S. Privateers could specify a Stage 1 rally kit which comprised different carburettor jets and chokes (160-170bhp) or a Stage 2 kit which added a through-flow exhaust system to the package and liberated 175bhp.

Porsche's first official rally programme added to the growing catalogue of 911 triumphs which included the European GT Rally championship, the Tulip Rally and the Geneva Rally (all Vic Elford/David Stone), the Austrian Alpine Rally and the Argentinian Grand Prix (Sobieslav Zasada).

SWEET TASTE OF SUCCESS

Still more pace and ability joined the 911's cause with the introduction of the 911R (for racing) mid-way through 1967. Only twenty-two 'Rs' were made, but the advantages they brought were worth having, lightened bodywork with glassfibre doors, front wings and engine cover, thinner windscreen glass and plastic side windows; no sound deadening, heating or rear seats. Weight was slashed to just 1,764lb (800kg) (a saving of around 507lb (230kg)) and you can rest assured that this made the very best use of the 210bhp/8,000rpm achieved by substituting the regular engine for the Carrera 901/22 (also known as 'Carrera 6') full-race unit first seen in Maglioli's 1965 Targa Florio 904.

It was a dynamite combination and notable successes ensued, including a victorious debut outing in the Marathon de la Route (an eighty-four-hour high-speed trial around the Nurburgring). Shrewdly, the winning car was equipped with Porsche's controversial four-speed, semi-automatic Sportomatic transmission and, thus, performed a valuable PR exercise for Porsche.

Thanks to vagaries of late-1960s homologation, 911s – 'L', 'T' and 'R' – infiltrated just about all forms of GT and touring competition between 1967 and 1969. Just a few of the wins over that period included the 1967 Spa 24-Hours touring car race (Gaban/Pedro) and the 1968 World Rally Championship.

The 911T, in particular, figured strongly in Porsche's 1969 rally programme with Bjorn Waldegaard and Lars Helmer collecting trophies for both the Monte Carlo and

Racers all – from right to left: the 1965 911 2.0 that competed in the Monte Carlo Rally, the awesome 'Moby Dick' 935 of 1978 and the 961 (circuit version of 959) that raced at Le Mans in 1987.

Swedish rallies, while Pauli Toivonen made short work of the opposition in the notoriously demanding Acropolis Rally.

WALK-OVER

Meanwhile, on the track, the Spa 24-Hours was beginning to look like a Porsche benefit, with 911s taking the first four places. GT class wins that year were earned at Daytona, Spa, the Nurburgring, the Targa Florio, Le Mans, Monza and at Zeltweg. Gérard Larrousse and Maurice Gelin were in cracking form with their 911R, first hoisting the laurels in the newly revived Tour de France and then the Tour de Corse, repeating the previous year's victory of Vic Elford.

As Production 911s became brawnier, so their racing counterparts tightened their stranglehold on the sport. The introduction of the fuel-injected 2.2-litre engine and, with it, a longer wheelbase for the 911, spawned the 240bhp 911ST with thinner sheet steel used for the roof and side panels, aluminium doors and glassfibre bumpers, front lid and wheelarch extensions. All the windows apart from the windscreen were made from Plexiglass and it almost goes without saying that all fripperies were banished: that included carpets, passenger sun visor, glove box lid and even underseal. All the paring was worth around 397lb (180kg), bringing the racing weight down to 1,852lb (840kg) – almost as light as the 911R.

With Waldegaard at the wheel, the ST

duly cleaned-up in the 1970 Monte Carlo Rally, bringing up Porsche's hat-trick in the event. Gérard Larrousse, driving a similar car, finished second. It really was Waldegaard's year for he went on to win the Swedish Rally outright for the second time. Moreover, he achieved the 'double-double' in a 911S. It was Porsche's year, too. Thanks to the efforts of Waldegaard (who added the Austrian Alpine Rally to his tally), Janger's victory in the Danube Rally and Claude Haldi's second place in the Lyon-Charbonnières event, Porsche walked off with the World Rally Championship.

Consummate performer as the 911ST was in rallies, it mustn't be overlooked that it took few prisoners on tarmac and was more than a force to be reckoned with in GT racing, winning its category in the World Championship long distance races with almost crushing authority.

UNBEARABLE LIGHTNESS OF BEING (BEATEN)

Porsche didn't always have things its own way. The factory really pulled out all the stops for Gérard Larrousse in the 1970 Tour de France, building him the lightest 911ST of all (several cases of champagne donated

Weissach is Porsche's 148-acre research and development facility and home to the competitions department.

911s were a common sight at the 1983 Monte Carlo Rally, if no longer dominant.

Smith and Smith-Haas in the 1984 Silverstone 1000km.

by Larrousse himself were riding on the outcome). Indeed, the outcome exceeded all expectations, with the Weissach mechanics shaving a remarkable 112lb (51kg) from the ST's already sylph-like 1,852lb (840kg). At 1,740lb (789kg), this was the lightest 911 that the factory had ever built. Many of the parts were made from titanium and, with 245bhp at 8,000rpm from a magnesium-blocked 2,395cc engine, the power-to-weight ratio was really quite formidable.

It wasn't good enough, though. Larrousse's ST had to give best to Matra's two V12 prototype racing cars which, despite early doubts over durability, captured the first two places.

Porsche also knew better than to slug it out with the little Alpine-Renaults in Europe in 1971, instead conserving their efforts for the Safari Rally. For this event, outright power wasn't as important as reliability and so the standard 180bhp engine was retained which, married to Monte Carlo ratios, limited top speed to around 112mph (180kph). What distinguished these cars, however, were their jacked-up suspensions which lent them a slightly comical 'on stilts' appearance.

The tall settings achieved the necessary ground clearance to deal with some of the toughest and most hostile rallying terrain in the world, but they didn't work very well in the event. Waldegaard retired after an excursion from the road and Ake Andersson having to quit with rear suspension problems.

Later on in the year, Waldegaard salvaged some pride for Porsche by finishing second overall in the RAC Rally, but that's the best the company did all year in rallying. In fact, it was the end of an era – the 911's pre-eminence in this field of the sport had come to a close, at least until the advent of a four-wheel drive Carrera in 1984, which won the Paris–Dakar rally and paved the way for a 959 to do the same the following year.

BACK TO WINNING WAYS

Things were a lot more encouraging on the track, though, with a whole stack of GT class wins falling to the Zuffenhausen marque. In fact, Porsche was moving into another dominant phase. With the regular 911 getting 2,341cc for 1972, the racers were bored-out to 2,492cc and could command 270bhp. The Kremer team was a rising force and, with driver John 'Fitz' Fitzpatrick, won the European Grand Touring Car Championship and the Porsche Cup. Success came in the United States, too, with Hurley Haywood winning the IMSA Camel GT Championship.

Better was still to come. Late in 1972, the Carrera RS and its racing derivative the RSR were unveiled at the Paris Show and these were to prove the most effective of all Porsche's homologated 911s.

The RSR, forty-nine of which were built, quickly established itself as *the* car to beat, a feat which few achieved over the next three years. The 1973 version carried a 2.8-litre engine with 'over 300bhp' and won all but two of the European GT rounds, the championship ending in a tie between Porsche drivers Clemens Schickentanz and Claude Ballot-Lena.

A measure of just how good the RSR was came with several outright victories in the World Championship rounds, an unprecedented achievement for Porsche's production-based racers. The Daytona 24 Hours was won by Peter Gregg and Hurley Haywood while, in Europe, factory drivers Herbert Mueller and Gijs van Lennep won the last Targa Florio round the Little Madonie circuit in Sicily – both historic achievements.

TURBO BLOWS IN

In many ways, the year 1974 was historic, too, for it marked the race track debut of the

This is the 1983 Monte Carlo Rally, with R Menghini driving a 930 TB.

911 Turbo, the development of which was the responsibility of Norbert Singer. This was just the boost (if you'll pardon the pun) the 911 needed, and the Turbo went on to dominate just about every race and championship in Europe.

The Turbo RSRs were used as a testbed for the Group 5 race cars which, in turn, evolved into the 934/935 Turbo. So much has already been written about the 935, that its record hardly needs repeating here, suffice it to say that it became the most successful Porsche competition car of all. Over the course of eight seasons, the 935 won no less than forty-two World Championship events and a staggering seventy IMSA championship races in the United States, a formidable record to hand on to the next generation 956 and 962 Group C/IMSA racers which in their turn duly carried on the good work from 1982–1983 onwards, still being powered by essentially the same production-based engine.

The 935's outstanding record reached a glorious climax in 1979, when a team Kremer Porsche Racing car driven by Klaus Ludwig and Don and Bill Whittington swept all aside at the Le Mans 24 Hours. This was the first time in years that the French classic had been won by a production-based car. Unless someone changes the rules, it will probably be the last time, too.

In Rallycross, just about anything goes, but few things go as well as a 911. Driven by D Atkinson, this one's competing in the 1987 British Rallycross Grand Prix.

911 in racing action.

Carrera RSR Turbo.

Carrera 2.7 Safari.

911: THE COMPETITION CARS

1965

911 2.0 'Monte'

1,991cc. 80/66mm bore/stroke. 9.8:1 cr. 160bhp.

Remarks

The 911 made its motorsport debut shortly after production began. For the Monte Carlo Rally, the 911 – homologated in the GT class – was mildly tuned for 160bhp, given a 100-litre (22-gallon) fuel tank, larger brakes and a limited-slip differential. Drivers Linge and Falk came fifth overall in this first effort.

1967

911S 2.0 'Rally'

1,991cc. 80/66mm bore/stroke. 10:1 cr. 170bhp.

Remarks

The 'Rally' version of the 911S. Painted polo red with black interior, standard equipment included heated rear window with wiper, tinted glass, reclining passenger (co-driver) seat, 100-litre (22-gallon) fuel tank, ambient temperature gauge and Koni dampers.

911R 2.0

1,991cc. 80/66mm bore/stroke. 10.5:1 cr. 210bhp.

Remarks

Competition car with Carrera 6 engine, built in small numbers specifically for motorsport. No spare fat so empty weight a lean 1,830lb (830kg).

1970

911S 2.2 'Rally'

2,195cc. 84/66mm bore/stroke. 9.8:1 cr. 180bhp.

Remarks

'Rally' version of 911S 2.2 scored victories in Monte Carlo Rally, Swedish Rally, RAC Rally and Austrian Alpine event. Gave Porsche World Rally Championship in 1970.

911S 2.3

2,247cc. 85/66mm bore/stroke. 10.3:1 cr. 240bhp.

Remarks

Circuit version of the 911S 2.2 with displacement increased by 52cc and maximum output increased to 240bhp. Equipped with two electric fuel pumps; six-piston, dual-row fuel injection; 7 (18) and 9in (22cm) forged alloy rims. Became a firm favourite with production sports car privateers in both circuit and endurance events.

911S 2.4 'Proto'

2,395cc. 85/70.5mm bore/stroke. 10.3:1 cr. 260bhp.

Remarks

Special ultra-lightweight 911ST for 1970 Tour de France. Empty weight 1,742lb (790kg). Engine breathed through two Weber triple-choke carburettors and used transistorised ignition.

1971

911S 2.2 'Safari'

2,195cc. 84/66mm bore/stroke. 9.8:1 cr. 180bhp.

Remarks

Special 911 with raised suspension for 1971 East African Safari rally.

1972

911S 2.5

2,492cc. 86.7/70.4mm bore/stroke. 10.3:1 cr. 270bhp.

Remarks

Limited run series for customers, price DM49,000. Replaced a year later by Carrera RS 2.7, respectively RS 3.0.

1973

911 Carrera RSR 2.8

2,800cc. 92/70.4mm bore/stroke. 10.3:1 cr. 300bhp.

Remarks

Group 4 race version of the RS 2.7. Usually entered privately, these Group 4 Carreras decided European GT Championship races between themselves, such was their domination of the series. They won seven of the nine events.

1973–1974

911 Carrera RSR 3.0

2,994cc. 95/70.4mm bore/stroke. 10.3:1 cr. 315/330bhp.

Remarks

Replacement for RSR 2.8. Fifty Carrera RS 3.0s were converted to RSRs for races and rallies. Greatest sporting successes: overall victory in the 1973 Targa Florio, European GT Championship, European GT Hillclimb Championship.

1974

911 Carrera RSR Turbo

2,142cc. 83/66mm bore/stroke. 6.5:1 cr. 450/500bhp.

Remarks

The RSR Turbo race car was built as a test bed for future production race cars to compete in Group 5. It was an important starting point and forerunner of the 935 Turbo which appeared two years later. Turbo was intercooled, injection mechanical. Drive to locked back axle via a five-speed gearbox. Top speed 300kph (186mph). Major successes: second at Le Mans and at the Watkins Glen 6 hours endurance race.

1976–1977

934 Turbo

2,994cc. 95/70.4mm bore/stroke. 6.5:1 cr. 485bhp.

Remarks

Superseded Carrera RSR 3.0. Race version of Germany's fastest production sports car. Built in limited numbers for private customers. Price: DM108,000. US 1977 version developed 540bhp.

935 Turbo

2,857cc. 92.8/70.4mm bore/stroke. 6.5:1 cr. 590bhp.

Remarks

Porsche's sports car for Group 5. Intercooled turbo, mechanical injection, locked back axle, four-speed gearbox. Top speed 340kph (211mph). With the 935, Porsche won the 1976 Manufacturers' World Championship and won again in 1977 with a modified 935 producing 630bhp.

1977

935 Turbo 'Baby'

1,425cc. 71/60mm bore/stroke. 6.5:1 cr. 320bhp.

Remarks

Special derivative of 935 to compete in Division II (up to 2 litres) of German Race Sport Championship. Weight 1,654lb (750kg). Competed in just two races and won one of them – at Hockenheim with Jacky Ickx driving.

1978

935/78 Turbo 'Moby Dick'

3,211cc. 95.8/74.4mm. 7.0:1 cr. 750bhp.
Remarks
The ultimate development of the 935 within Group 5 regulations, 'Moby Dick' had a radically modified body for better aerodynamics, water-cooled cylinder heads, four valves per cylinder and four overhead camshafts. The 935/78 goes down in the record books as the fastest and most powerful 911 of all.

911 SC 'Safari'

2,994cc. 95/70.4mm bore/stroke. 9.1:1 cr. 250bhp.
Remarks
Porsche's works entry in the 26th East Africa Safari rally. Used mechanical fuel injection, limited slip differential and jacked-up suspension with 28cm ground clearance. Finished second and fourth overall.

1984

911 Carrera 4×4 'Paris–Dakar'

3,164cc. 95/74.4mm bore/stroke. 9.5:1 cr. 225bhp.
Remarks
Porsche 911 Carrera adapted to special conditions of the Paris–Dakar rally with all-wheel drive. Doors, front and rear lids and bumpers in plastic. Tank capacity 260 litres. Result: first, sixth and twenty-sixth. Porsche collected team prize.

911 SC/RS

2,994cc. 95/70.4mm bore/stroke. 10.3:1 cr. 255bhp.
Remarks
Customer demand for a car that could be both road registered and used in international events, mostly rallies, was satisfied by this evolution series of just twenty units. Changes from standard specification included mechanical fuel injection, a forty per cent limited slip differential, front wings, doors and boot lid in aluminium, bumpers and front spoiler in glass reinforced plastic.

1985–1986

959 'Paris–Dakar'

1985: 3,164cc. 95/74.4mm bore/stroke. 9.5:1 cr. 230bhp. 1986: 2,847cc. 95/67mm bore/stroke. 8.0:1 cr. 400bhp.
Remarks
Following an inauspicious debut in 1985, the Paris–Dakar rally fell to the four-wheel drive 959 in 1986. The three 959s entered finished the gruelling trial in first, second and sixth positions.

1986–1987

961

2,847cc. 95/67 bore/stroke. 9.0:1 cr. 640/650bhp.
Remarks
Circuit version of the 959. Two turbos with intercooling, four valves per cylinder, water-cooled cylinder heads, electronically controlled injection and ignition (Bosch Motronic), electronically-controlled four-wheel drive, six-speed gearbox. Weight 2,536lb (1,150kg), top speed 342kph (212mph). Race entries: Le Mans 1986, Daytona 1987, Le Mans 1987.

6 Hot the Wind Blows

Porsche knew how to make turbocharging work and used it to slay the giants of Can–Am racing. By this time, the legendary 5-litre, flat-twelve 917 had been outlawed by the FIA from competing in Europe. But it was far from finished as a race car.

Jo Siffert was already on the scene with the 917PA but Porsche knew that to conquer the awesome 8.1-litre Chevrolet-powered McLarens, the 917 would require more power still. Eventually the 917/30 was good for at least 1,000bhp and had earned the tag 'the ultimate racing car' from driver Brian Redman.

The golden years for the 917 were 1972 and 1973 when the Porsches of the Penske team crushed McLaren clean out of the Can–Am frame. Porsche domination would almost certainly have continued but for the intervention of the fuel crisis, a force more powerful even than the FIA, which brought the profligacies of Can–Am to a close.

Thus circumstances contrived to channel Porsche's energies into the World Championship for endurance racing and the 911 was back in business. The new strategy was formulated to take advantage of the fact that, from 1976, the World Championship for Manufacturers would be based on production cars, leaving the World Sportscar Championship for up to 3-litre prototypes.

THE TURBO FACTOR

At the 1974 Le Mans trials, it was a turbocharged 911 waving the Porsche flag. The 911 Carrera Turbo was based on the successful RSR but with its engine capacity reduced to 2,142cc, so that when it was subjected to the multiplication factor of 1.4 (the figure the FIA applied to supercharged or turbocharged engines) its capacity would remain within the 3-litre limit, albeit by 1cc. The regular 2-litre crankshaft reduced the stroke to 66mm and the bore was reduced to 83mm.

With the single KKK (Kuhnle, Kopp and Kausch) turbocharger delivering 1.4bar boost, the Bosch-injected flat-six developed 516bhp and 406lb ft of torque – impressive outputs by any standards. Certainly too impressive for the type 915 gearbox which failed at Le Mans in 1974, robbing the car of possible victory. In the event, it finished second to the Matra–Simca V12, so the debut outing was by no means a disaster.

The production 911 Turbo was, perhaps, *the* sensation of the 1974 Paris Show, and little wonder. Almost double the price of the 911 2.7, the 930 (as it was known internally) carried a full 3 litres of turbocharged flat-six, a luxury equipment list with air conditioning, electric windows and leather trim and 155mph (249kph) performance.

A NEW BREED

This was the car that proved the adage 'racing improves the breed', the car that owed its very existence to a successful racing programme. The ultimate development of this cross-pollination was the 3.3-litre ver-

(Above and right): *Original 3-litre 911 Turbo developed 260bhp and 254lb ft of torque. The top speed was around 155mph and it could accelerate from rest to 60mph in comfortably under six seconds.*

sion of the Turbo which replaced the 3-litre car four years later. Naturally, the motoring press was impressed . . .

'The acceleration is simply breathtaking and the maximum speed very high but the real achievement of the Turbo is its practicality.' The praise was gushing, but this was 1978 and, as every reader of *Motor* magazine knew, the arrival of the ultimate Porsche 911 was an event not to be taken lightly.

For lovers of the 911, the test was vindication of something they'd known all along – that the rear-engined Porsche remained more than a match for its supercar peers some fifteen years after its momentous debut at the Frankfurt Motor Show. Like the Deux Chevaux and the Mini, the 911 was a survivor, a design that transcended normal production values and trends.

The Turbo itself had already survived for four years after a somewhat shaky start. The actual car exhibited at the 1974 Paris Salon had more than a few loose ends that took a surprisingly long time to tie. It boasted cross-drilled disc brakes, for instance, which looked fabulous but wouldn't

be put into production until the 3.3-litre model was introduced in 1978. Back in 1974, the factory was still battling with hairline cracking. Perhaps more worrying was the Paris car's wooden mock-up turbocharger tract! Come the Geneva Show the following March, the four-speed 930 type transmission had yet to be granted the final thumbs-up so the handful of journalists who were allowed to drive prototypes on the roads around Geneva did so on the understanding that they didn't try any impromptu standing starts.

By April, however, the Turbo was ready to roll and, over the next five months, 273 cars had found their way into European homes. The Turbo's initial UK price was £14,740 and, despite the onerous repercussions of the fuel crisis, the queue was seventeen customers long.

CRISIS, WHAT CRISIS?

Indeed, the very existence of the 911 Turbo in such a depressed economic climate must go down as one of Porsche's more courageous acts of faith. Dr Fuhrmann was the man with his hand on the green light button, the man who would have to justify the lifestyle of a supercar with potentially extravagant habits. There's no question now that the very idea of the Turbo made some of Porsche's luminaries very nervous. It was sug-

911 Turbo SE Cabriolet – already a blue chip investment.

911 Turbo SE – value in late 1989 was £150,000 and climbing.

(Left): *First among equals. 911 Turbo SE squares up against Testarossa, Zagato and Countach.*

The Turbo SE's interior verged on the extravagant but remained tasteful.

Rear wing for the 3.3 Turbo provided more effective engine cooling, especially to the intercooler.

gested, at one point, that just the 400 necessary for homologation purposes should be made. Given Porsche's record of limited-run race 'specials', the notion clearly had a strong precedent.

But Fuhrmann saw the Turbo as something greater, a car for wealthy and discerning customers to use day in, day out. And, of course, he was right. In deciding that the Turbo should be a full production model, he argued the philosophy that has kept many a supercar maker in business, which was simply this: as long as there are cars, there will always be people who will want something that is better and faster. Nailing his emotional colours to the mast, the man who was

also responsible for the 928 then went on to say that possibly the last car ever made would be a sports car.

That Fuhrmann was a dyed-in-the-wool enthusiast for the breed no one could have doubted when, having listened to criticisms levelled at what some saw to be the Turbo body's excessive girth, he had the Turbo's engine and running gear fitted to a standard 'narrow body' Carrera bodyshell for his personal use and ended up with a car that was 6mph (10kph) faster than the Turbo.

It's a pity that this option was never offered. The Turbo body with normally-aspirated Carrera engine – a combination offered some years later – rather missed the point.

The Turbo was instantly recognisable with its flared flanks and asymetrically-sized wheels and tyres. This is a 1979 3.3.

3.3 Turbo was crowned the 'world's fastest-accelerating production car' in a speed trial at North Weald Aerodrome.

Special light-alloy wheels for the SE.

*Turbocharged 3.3-litre flat-six looks
standard but develops an extra
30bhp.*

911 Turbo SE – as practical as the first 911.

911 Turbo 3.3 Cabriolet was introduced for 1988 model year.

As already mentioned, the Turbo's engine was a logical development of the Carrera 3-litre unit that had done Porsche so many favours on the track. Dimensionally, nothing had changed – 95/70.4mm bore/stroke gave the same swept volume of 2,994cc. The aluminium block with its Nikasil liners was the same, too. One clear difference, however, was the use of flat-top forged pistons to drop the compression ratio to 6.5:1 for turbocharging. At full boost the effective compression ratio would soar to 11.5:1.

HOT MUSTARD

The stalwart mechanical fuel injection that had seen 'hot' 911s through thick and thin finally threw in the towel in favour of Bosch's new, 'cleaner' and more accurate K-Jetronic system. Likewise, contact-breaker ignition was supplanted by 'maintenance-free' electronic.

The KKK turbo, sited just behind the left side of the number plate valance, was wastegate-governed to a maximum boost pressure of 0.8bar at 3,000 revs. Thus equipped, the 3-litre engine developed 260bhp at 5,500rpm and 286lb ft of torque at 4,000rpm. When *Motor* magazine tested the car in 1975 it recorded a top speed of 150mph and a 0–60mph (0–96.5kph) time of 6.1secs: nothing to get too worked up about by 959 standards, but hot mustard in 1975.

It's often been wondered why the Turbo started off with a four-speed gearbox when its peaky engine characteristics cried out for a fifth speed. The answer is that the wider teeth of the four-speed transmission (type 930) were better able to cope with the extra

TECHNICAL FILE   Porsche 911 3.3 Turbo

Engine: 3,299cc (3.3-litre) air-cooled flat-six with chain-driven overhead cam-
               shafts. Fuel supply by Bosch K-Jetronic fuel injection; turbocharger;
               intercooler.

Perfor-   161mph (259kph) top speed, 0–60mph (0–96.5kph) in 5.3 seconds,
mance: 16mpg. Peak power 300bhp at 5,500rpm, peak torque 303lb ft at
               4,000rpm.

torque generated by the turbo. The older 915 five-speed box simply wasn't up to the job. So strong was the four-speeder, in fact, that it was easily able to deal with the 750bhp of the 935/78 racer.

A beefier clutch (up in diameter from 225 to 240mm) and alterations to the suspension to give firmer control were also part of the Turbo specification.

Sales of the Turbo more than justified Furhmann's faith in the project. Production peaked in 1977 with 1,722 examples being built. And in the following year, Porsche introduced a still more powerful engine for the car with cubic capacity increased to 3,299cc by means of boring and stroking (97/74.4mm). The compression ratio was raised to 7.0:1 and more power liberated by an air-to-air intercooler which reduced the temperature of the air charge by 50 to 60deg C before it entered the manifold. To feed the intercooler with the gulps of air it required, Porsche granted the new car a bigger rear wing with special ducting for that very purpose.

THE BIG TIME

With this model, the engine outputs jumped to 300bhp and 304lb ft of torque with corresponding improvements in top speed acceleration. The *Motor* test of the 3.3 left no one in any doubt that the Turbo had now entered the ranks of the supercar 'greats'. Of the performance, it said:

'Porsche claims that the top speed is in excess of 260kph, which is 161.6mph. We could not *quite* match that (perhaps because we did not fold the door mirror flat), but our mean speed of 160.1mph should satisfy most owners. It also happens to be the highest top speed we have ever measured for a production model.

'The acceleration is startling. For our MIRA starts we were dropping the clutch abruptly at 6,000rpm, leaving two expensive black lines of rubber on the road for a considerable distance. After only 2.2secs, the car was travelling at 30mph, 40mph came up in 2.7secs, 50 in 3.7secs, 60 in 5.3secs. This last figure and the 0–100mph time of 12.3secs also break new ground, making the Turbo the quickest production car we (and, as far as we know, anyone else) have ever tested. The standing quarter-mile is covered in 13.4secs, passing the post at 104mph.'

I was a callow road tester with *Motor* at the time and well remember being told that the Turbo was strictly out of bounds. I think 'insane' was the word editor Tony Curtis used to describe the Porsche's performance.

Alfresco acceleration: the author at the wheel of a 911 Turbo Cabriolet.

911 3.3 TURBO – THE VITAL STATISTICS

Length	168.9in/4,290mm
Width	69.9in/1,775mm
Height	51.6in/1,310mm
Wheelbase	89.5in/2,272mm
Front track	56.4in/1,432mm
Rear track	59.1in/1,501mm
Turning circle	33ft 11in
Boot capacity	4.3cu ft
Engine	6 cylinder, horizontally opposed
Capacity	3,229cc
Bore	97mm
Stroke	74.4mm
Compression	7.0:1
Valvegear	Overhead camshaft, 2 valves per cylinder
Ignition	Electronic
Fuel	Bosch K-Jetronic fuel injection. Turbocharger
Max power	300bhp/5,500rpm
Max torque	317lb ft/4,000rpm
Transmission	5-speed, manual
Maxima at 6,750rpm:	1st 45mph
	2nd 78mph
	3rd 110mph
	4th 144mph
Suspension	
Front	Independent by MacPherson struts, torsion bars, telescopic dampers and anti-roll bar
Rear	Independent by semi-trailing arms, torsion bars, telescopic dampers and anti-roll bar
Brakes	
Front	11.1in (282.5mm) diameter vent discs
Rear	11.4in (290mm) diameter discs
Wheels	Forged alloy 7/9in rims
Tyres	BF Goodrich Comp T/A, 205/55ZR16 front, 245/45ZR16 rear
Performance	
Max speed	158mph
0–60mph	4.9secs
0–100mph	12.1secs
0–130mph	22.7secs
30–70mph	4.3secs
30–50mph/4th	7.6secs
50–70mph/5th	8.6secs
Standing ¼ mile	13.1secs/106mph
Standing km	24.1secs/134mph
Overall mpg	16.6
Fuel grade	4-star (97RM)
Tank capacity	18.7 gallons (85 litres)
Weight	
Kerb	3,051lb/1,385kg
Distribution	42/58 per cent front/rear
Max payload	707lb/320kg
Max towing weight	1,768lb/800kg

Figures courtesy of Porsche GB Ltd and *Autocar & Motor* magazine.

SMOOTHER OPERATOR

In typically thorough fashion, the 3.3 wasn't merely a 3-litre with more grunt. Various aspects of the specification had been changed to make the new car every bit as roadworthy as its predecessor, and probably more so. The clutch plate was redesigned for a smoother take-up and to reduce gearbox 'chatter' at low speeds. A small point maybe but something that required the engine to be moved back three centimetres. In common with the SC, the 3.3 Turbo was equipped with a brake servo, and a good one at that: it lightened the load without removing the feel. On the subject of brakes, the 3.3 became the actual recipient of the Porsche-designed Alcan calipers and type 917 cross-drilled discs that the original 1974 3-litre car should have had all along, and what a difference they made. The Turbo's braking performance was suddenly catapulted into the track car league.

The 3.3-litre Turbo was swifter than any of its 911 predecessors and, indeed, as rapid as anything before the advent of cars like the 959 and Ferrari F40. If it was no quicker than a hot hatchback on a twisty back-route, it at least had the measure of its wider, mid-engined supercar peers similarly constrained. Whatever may be said about the Turbo's handling – and because of the sudden boost characteristics, gross bad behaviour was always a possibility – the sheer compactness and manageability of the car should never be underestimated. The joy of the Turbo was the breathtaking extent of its ability; the relentless neck-straining acceleration, the inimitably visceral exhaust note and the wonderfully communicative steering. To dwell too long on the dark side of the Turbo's make-up was to miss the point. 'In our opinion,' concluded the *Motor* test, 'the 911 Turbo is probably the best example of precision engineering on four wheels.' It's hard to argue with that.

CLUB SPORT *vs* 911 CARRERA 2.7 RS *vs* TURBO 3.3

	CS	RS	TURBO
MAXIMUM SPEED			
mph	152.1	150(est)	158
ACCELERATION FROM REST			
mph	sec	sec	sec
0–30	2.0	2.1	1.9
0–40	2.7	3.1	2.6
0–50	4.0	4.2	3.8
0–60	5.1	5.5	4.9
0–70	7.0	7.6	6.2
0–80	8.7	9.4	8.2
0–90	10.5	11.6	9.9
0–100	13.1	14.9	12.1
0–110	16.0	18.8	15.2
0–120	19.6	23.4	18.5
IN TOP			
20–40	8.1	–	11.6
30–50	7.1	–	10.6
40–60	7.1	9.2	10.1
50–70	7.4	9.6	8.6
60–80	7.6	9.0	7.0
70–90	8.2	8.6	6.3
80–100	8.7	9.5	6.4
90–110	8.8	11.3	7.0
IN FOURTH			
20–40	5.6	–	8.5
30–50	5.3	6.5	7.6
40–60	5.4	6.2	6.2
50–70	5.6	5.7	4.7
60–80	5.4	5.2	4.3
70–90	5.1	5.5	4.4
80–100	5.1	6.1	4.6
90–110	5.5	6.1	5.0
FUEL CONSUMPTION			
Overall mpg	19.9	16.7	16.6

7 Greased Lightning

Porsche's phenomenal record of success on the world's race tracks may have had its *real world* expression in cars like the 911 Turbo and 959, but that hasn't been enough for some enthusiasts. In particular, the all-conquering 935 – based closely on the production 911 Turbo right down to its floorpan, rear suspension and basic engine components – has evoked many a fantasy, some of which have ended up as road-going realities.

Most of these 'specials' have lightened flat-nose bodies with shark-gill bonnet louvres, impossibly wide tyres, 'sprint' gearing and mechanical modifications that allow even more fuel to be crammed into the engine by the turbocharger. Usually the objective is to achieve the undeniably sexy 935 look rather than its crushing performance since even a mildly re-worked 3.3-litre Turbo engine is mighty potent.

But some have gone for broke. German tuners have long recognised the 911's potential and, back in 1987, three of them – Ruf, RS Tuning and Koenig – sent their toughest street fighters to VW's fabulous Ehra–Lessien proving ground near Wolfsburg in northern Germany to slug it out with five other of the world's fastest cars in a specially organised showdown attended by former colleague Paul Frère, *Motor* magazine's then European correspondent.

TOWARDS 200mph

Ehra–Lessien is 15.5 miles (25 kilometres) round, with a pair of high bankings joined by two 6.2-mile (10-kilometre) straights. It's the only track in Europe suitable for determining the absolute top speed of a 200mph (322kph) car. Frère sets the scene: 'We gathered the nine fastest production cars in the world – cars with names that do not come more emotive. Not one, but two Porsche 959s; two Ferraris – a GTO and Testarossa; a Lamborghini Countach; an Isdera Imperator; an AMG 560E; and three highly-tuned Porsche 911 Turbos from Ruf, RS Tuning and Koenig.'

The AMG was, in fact, the famous 'Hammer' – 5.6 litres and 360bhp of quad-cam modified Benz V8 wrapped up in the sober and self-effacing shape of Mercedes' W124-series saloon. The word was that this king among Q-cars wouldn't stop accelerating until the far side of 180mph (289kph), but even that wouldn't be good enough in the company of the Porsches. And nor would the identically-powered Isdera's best shot, despite its much sleeker body.

The Koenig, for instance, looked formidable. Based on the inevitable 911 Turbo, this projectile carried 935-sized wheel arch extensions to accommodate gumball rear tyres on 16×13in (40×33mm) rims. The RS (Reinhold Schmirler) 911 shared a similar specification and both were developed by Swiss Pierre Ofzky, a one-time employee of Ruf. The Koenig car used the standard Porsche four-speed gearbox, but the RS car had a Ruf five-speeder.

As for Alois Ruf himself, he'd brought along an even more extreme – though remarkably standard-looking – development of the 911 theme powered by a 3.4-litre, twin-turbo version of the Porsche flat-six said to develop 469bhp and driving through Ruf's own five-speed gearbox. Frère explains what made the Ruf car special:

'The Ruf runs on special 17-inch diameter wheels and the special Dunlop D40 tyres originally developed for the 959. Its body is lightened by using light-weight sports seats, aluminium front wings and a bonnet and front and rear bumpers made of plastic material. 'A special air dam with a central opening for the oil cooler is integrated into the front bumper. At the rear, the standard Carrera (not the higher and rather ugly Turbo) spoiler is used and the external mirror is replaced with a smaller and better streamlined one.

Apart from the rather inconspicuous front air dam, what really gives the car away are the two large intakes just behind the top of the rear wheels, which feed air to the twin intercoolers. In addition, the car is slightly lowered, the suspension is stiffened up – but not to an unacceptable extent – and the car is fitted with special brakes, developed by Ruf and apparently similar to the 959 brakes. With no frills, but finished in bright yellow, the lowered car was supremely elegant and its performance certainly did not belie its promise.'

RAPID RIVALS

Frère's first drive was in that other 'legend' of the supercar set, the Lamborghini Coun-

RS Tuning 911 Turbo – when standard isn't fast enough.

The road to racing success starts here – at the Porsche Research Centre at Weissach.

tach QV. The track was still damp from early morning rain but the Lamborghini felt good and stable and his foot was soon flat to the floor. The initial two-way runs through the timing lights gave the outlandish Countach an average speed of 175mph (281kph), but the track was still wet and the Italian car's huge rear tyres were kicking up vast clouds of spray. Later on in the day it managed a mean maximum of 179mph (288kph) – thrilling stuff, but a far cry from the factory's 190mph (306kph) claim.

The Lamborghini's great rival, the Ferrari Testarossa, did rather better in the top speed tests, recording a maximum of 185.3mph (298kph). Frère found the con-trasts between the two Italian thorough-breds to be marked and fascinating: 'The Ferrari felt the more practical car, with the side windows opening properly and more space for luggage and oddments. Except for the rather stiff gearchange – typically Ferrari – driving it does not require much brute force and it felt beautifully stable in the adverse conditions.'

Against all expectations, the other Ferrari in the exercise – the exquisitely pro-portioned GTO – proved slower than the Testarossa, recording exactly the same speed as the Countach: 179mph (288kph). Suspicions that all might not be well were confirmed when one of its ignition 'black boxes' packed up and retired one of the cylinder banks soon after the top speed runs. Even so, the GTO still managed to beat the Isdera's 176mph (283kph). This posed another paradox since the like-engined but boxier AMG 'Hammer' (with automatic transmission!) went on to record a startling maximum of 182.5mph (293kph). Frère was clearly and understandably impressed:

'Imagine a spacious and very civilised looking four-door automatic doing well over 180mph! This was the only front-engined car of the lot and it felt utterly stable at speed, wet or dry, though the standard Daimler–Benz power steering was not quite up to the speed and felt a bit vague around the straight ahead position.

'But don't for a minute imagine that the automatic transmission makes it all so easy to get good acceleration figures: floor the throttle and the car will be left standing in a cloud of rubber smoke with the rear wheels spinning wildly. In fact, the torque converter makes it particularly difficult to feather the accelerator accurately to

SPECIFICATION	Porsche 959S	Porsche 959 Confort	Ruf-Porsche 911 Turbo	RS Porsche 911 Turbo	AMG Mercedes 560E Auto
Price	est £140,000	est £140,000	£85,000	£79,200	£66,400
Engine	twin turbo 6	twin turbo 6	twin turbo 6	twin turbo 6	V8
Bhp/rpm	450 @ 6500	450 @ 6500	469 @ 6100	520 @ na	355 @ 5500
Torque lb ft/rpm	370 @ 5500	370 @ 5500	457 @ 5400	na	390 @ 4500
Transmission	6-sp man	6-sp man	5-sp man	5-sp man	4-sp auto

SPECIFICATION	Ferrari Testarossa	Isdera Imp 108i	Lamborghini Countach	Ferrari GTO
Price	£84,500	£81,300	£82,200	est £100,000
Engine	flat-12	V8	V12	V8
Bhp/rpm	380 @ 5750	390 @ 5500	455 @ 7000	400 @ 7000
Torque lb ft/rpm	354 @ 4500	387 @ 4100	368 @ 5000	366 @ 3800
Transmission	5-sp man	5-sp man	5-sp man	5-sp man

PERFORMANCE	Porsche 959S	Porsche 959 Confort	Ruf-Porsche 911 Turbo (specialist cars)	RS Porsche 911 Turbo	AMG-Mercedes 560E Auto
Max speed (mph)	197.0	195.0	211.5	201.0	183.0
0–60 mph (sec)	3.6	4.0	4.0	4.0	5.2
0–100 mph (sec)	8.2	9.4	7.3	7.2	11.5
Stdg ¼ mile (sec)	11.9	12.3	11.7	11.6	13.6
Speed at end (mph)	119.5	116.0	133.5	133.5	109.5
Stdg km (sec)	21.7	22.2	–	–	–

PERFORMANCE	Ferrari Testarossa	Isdera Imp 108i	Lamborghini Countach	Ferrari GTO
Max speed (mph)	185.0	176.0	179.0	179.0
0–60 mph (sec)	5.4	5.0	4.7	5.0
0–100 mph (sec)	10.9	10.8	10.8	11.0
Stdg ¼ mile (sec)	13.7	13.3	12.9	14.1
Speed at end (mph)	111.0	111.0	110.0	113.0
Stdg km (sec)	–	–	–	–

Chevrolet Corvette – even faster than the fastest 911 if you've got enough litres.

Engine plumbing courtesy of RS Tuning.

The 935 'look' was often transposed on to road cars, with varying
results. The road car was merely posing in a car park, the racer
was competing in the 1984 Silverstone 1,000km.

make a good start and I tried several times before I was satisfied with mine. But then, the time over the quarter mile – 13.6 seconds – was one tenth better than I had achieved with the Testarossa!'

SHOWDOWN

Perhaps more predictably, the Porsches were the stars of the event, though again, there were some surprises in store. First out on the track were the 959s which breezed through the traps at a cool 195mph (314kph) and 197mph (316kph) respectively. Frère put the difference down to the fact that one of the 959s was a 'Sport' and therefore had only one external mirror. But what was to follow turned out to be truly remarkable. Both 959s were comprehensively beaten by the Ruf 911. Frère takes up the story:

'Setting off from the car park, there was a colossal push in the back and the wheels started to spin on the still damp surface. I had just gone into fifth gear when we passed the display, perhaps a mile away from our starting point, and I could hardly believe my eyes when it showed 311.9kph – 193.8mph! So on round the banking – where the car felt completely stable – and into the opposite straight, accelerator hard down on the floor. Result – 336.1kph, or 208.8mph, soon confirmed by 338 kph (210.1mph) on the opposite leg. And all this on a still damp track with the car raising a cloud of spray. When the surface had dried completely, ex-Ferrari racer Phil Hill – the other driver for the event – took the car out again and it went even faster, averaging 210.5mph, with a one-way speed of 211.2mph'.

The prospect of still higher speeds was entertained, albeit briefly, by the RS 911. The engine of this flat nose 935 look-alike was said to develop a staggering 520bhp and, indeed, the early signs were encouraging with a practice run through the timing beams at a comfortable 201mph (323kph). But before the serious action commenced a fan belt snapped with Frère at the wheel. Frère recalls: 'Fortunately, I spotted the red light on the dash panel immediately and no damage was done.

'I felt almost relieved when it came on, as the tyres were not properly balanced and caused considerable vibration – a fact that did not inspire much confidence. Proof, however, that the engine had suffered no damage was given two days later, when the car beat all comers in the acceleration tests.'

THE DRAG

Regrettably though, perhaps, not all that surprisingly, the Koenig 911 wasn't present for part two of the performance trial. It had blown a head gasket before even its top speed could be ascertained and was never seen again.

The venue for the acceleration tests was a sunny Hockenheim circuit, the longest straight of which was just long enough to accurately measure acceleration up to a quarter mile – long enough for two of the cars to reach 133.5mph (215kph).

Slowest – or least pulverisingly rapid – of the cars over this distance was the Testarossa which turned in a best time of 13.7 seconds. The Isdera was just 0.4 seconds quicker but recorded an identical 111mph (178kph) terminal speed. The Lamborghini felt more at home in the sprint stakes, blasting dramatically off the line to record an impressive 12.9 seconds. More amazing to many, though, was the AMG which, despite its four doors, big boot and automatic transmission put away a 13.6 second run.

The test track where Porsche discovered they had got it right . . .

But this part of the event was surely to be a 959 benefit. Four-wheel drive action had to play a major role here. Frère was the right man to be behind the wheel:

'I revved the engine to 7000, engaged low first and slipped my foot sideways to the left, off the clutch pedal. The car leapt forward, all four wheels spinning for a short period, and almost immediately, I had to change up – fortunately just a matter of pulling the lever straight back. Result – 12.3secs for the quarter mile. And this was the Confort model!

'Out of respect for such an expensive jewel, I politely suggested that the works driver who had driven the car from Stuttgart that morning should be responsible for putting the Sport version through its paces, which he did to such good effect that he broke the 12-second barrier: 11.9 seconds and an amazing 0–60mph (96.5kph) time of 3.6 seconds – 0.4 seconds quicker than I had achieved with the Confort.'

PHENOMENAL

Heady stuff. But the Ruf and RS were still to come and it didn't seem likely they'd disappoint. In fact, the results were simply staggering. This time, it was the RS that held a slight advantage, achieving a best time over the quarter mile of 11.6 seconds against the Ruf's 11.7 seconds. But both cars speared the timing beam at exactly the same speed – 133.5mph (215kph) or some 14mph faster than the quicker of the two 959s. This is all the more remarkable when you consider that the 911s had to claw back the ground initially lost to the 959s with their phenomenal four-wheel drive traction before blasting past. At 60mph (96.5kph), for example, the 959 Sport was still some 0.4

Strosek's 935 lookalike doesn't take imitation too seriously.

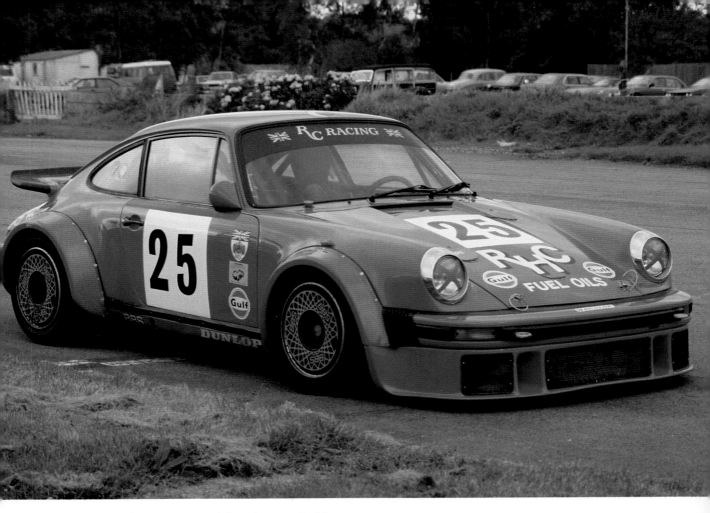

935 – one of the most successful racing cars in history.

seconds ahead of the hard-charging RS and Ruf, neither of which could quite crack the four-second barrier.

So . . . the 959 humbled by a 'mere' 911. Well, not quite. These cars were built for pure performance – to realise that 935 dream on the road. Either could be used as day-to-day transport but neither would offer anything like the levels of comfort, tractability or handling security of a 959, especially on wet or slippery roads.

Ohio, Transportation Research Center 7½-mile banked oval track (1987)
Ruf Porsche 911 – twin turbo
Averaged 202.5mph
3.3-litre flat-six, 646bhp at 7,500rpm. Five-speed manual gearbox, Goodyear Eagle racing tyres, 23.5 × 10.5–16 (front) and 25.5 × 12.5–16 (rear), 2,610lbs.

911 TURBO vs FERRARI TESTAROSSA

	911	Testa-rossa
cc	3,299	4,942
Max bhp	300	390
Max lb ft	317	362
Max mph	158	171
0–60 secs	4.9	5.2
30–70 secs	4.3	4.1
¼ mile	13.1	13.5
30–50 secs	7.6	5.1
50–70 secs	8.6	7.4
Overall mpg	16.6	16.6
Touring mpg	21.9	16.3
Mph/1,000rpm	27.4	26.5
Weight lb	3,051	3,675

8 The Great 911s

911. The hardest car in the world to approach with an open mind. More than a mere car, the Porsche 911 is a media phenomenon – a subject with the staying power of the British weather and the magnetic fascination of another Sinatra comeback. Each successive model year prolongs an automotive soap opera that's been running for twenty-seven years at or near the top of the ratings but the plot of which defies analysis. Porsche, who gave up trying to understand the 911's allure long ago, attempted to axe it, but the public wouldn't let it die. The 911 is the *LA Law* of editorial scheduling: just the presence of the perpetual Porsche's digital nomenclature can add a chromium sparkle to an otherwise jaded magazine cover.

Perhaps more significantly, the 911's enigmatic profile is infinitely exploitable. Treated with contrived irreverence, controversy is guaranteed. Conversely, it's a relatively simple matter to present the 911 as the best thing since Bardot at her best and prepare for a flood of fan mail. Either way, it's hard for the writer to lose and impossible for the reader to win. Those fortunate enough to own a 911 know the enigma best and, what's more, they voted for it with their bank balances. The critic's best shot is to arm himself with as much objectivity as a good yarn will allow and hope that the 911 doesn't tap that polemic whirlpool which will inevitably drag him into the '911 is magic/never was any good' syndrome.

Then again, the 911 doesn't have weaknesses in the accepted sense. The enigma is the challenge it represents and a set of virtues that it alone possesses. It's an old-fashioned car built to the highest standards and powered by an all-time great engine.

THEY STAND ALONE

But which are the *great* 911s, the ones that stand out like an exceptional wine in a good year? It's a question surrounded by as much controversy as the car itself. To the truly smitten, each and every model has been touched by genius, but few would disagree that the 2.7-litre Carrera RS introduced in 1972 was probably the most inspired road-going 911 of all. I remember the thrill of driving a well-cared-for 1973 example from London to Inverness one cold and crisp winter's day many years ago. The story of that drive appears later in this chapter.

What of the Turbo, though? There was a car to stir the soul. The standard Turbo had never been an easy car to get to grips with, let alone master. Its breathtaking straight-line performance was, regrettably, delivered in a succession of on-boost surges. If one of those surges happened to coincide with a tight, greasy bend, you could suddenly be charting your progress through the side window or, worse still, the side of a hedge.

Even with the five-speed version, produced right at the end of the Turbo's production life, Porsche missed a golden opportunity to temper the Turbo's tempestuous behaviour. Quite why the company didn't use the luxury of an extra gear to stack the intermediate ratios closer and thus reduce the worst effects of the turbo lag remains a mystery. *In extremis* the Turbo was about as friendly as a rattlesnake.

The flat-nose Turbo SE – with its, to some eyes, grotesquely embellished shape and extravagantly trimmed and appointed cabin – was much the same, of course – tantalisingly brilliant and terminally treacherous.

The Carrera 4's all-drive chassis made the 911 fit for the 1990s and beyond.

A great 911.

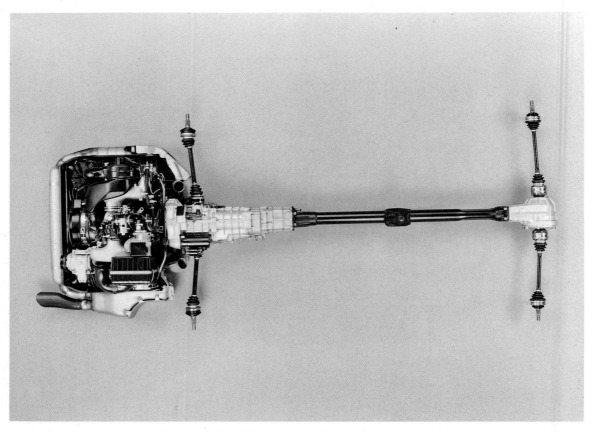

Carrera 4 drivetrain – sophisticated 4wd, if not as complex as the 959's system.

Yet there was something about it – its sheer audacity, the extra 30bhp, I've never been sure – that made it immensely likeable. The one I drove was a deep metallic blue with a scarlet leather cabin. Photographer Rich Newton, who came along for the ride, had just returned from a shoot in Modena with the quattrovalvole version of Lamborghini's Countach. The first time I gave the SE the gun in second, Newton fell silent mid-sentence; he wasn't frightened, merely comparing notes. His verdict was delivered almost immediately. The Porsche felt quicker, definitely quicker. Having driven the Countach myself barely six months earlier, I could but agree . . .

PORSCHE 911 TURBO SE

The flat nosed 911 – aesthetic parallels with the racing 935 were not coincidental – cost more than £80,000 when it went on sale in Britain in 1986 and was *very* exclusive. No more than a handful found their way into British homes, thus upstaging Aston's fifty-strong production run for the Zagato. Interestingly, both cars were dedicated oddballs: neither slotted into a readily definable category.

Simultaneously, the SE Turbo was both beguilingly old-fashioned (rear-slung engine, rear drive) and state-of-the-art (micro-managed and intercooled turbo, cross-drilled disc brakes with twin-pot calipers). The split personality wasn't a problem, in this case, more the hot-spot of the Porsche's appeal. The curious magic never strayed too far from the driver: his environment was almost too plush, the gold Porsche shields crowning the steering wheel boss and gear knob – both red and leather like the rest of our test car's cabin – teetering on the brink of bad taste, yet the sheer quality and craftsmanship of the fittings lifting the whole effect to dizzy heights.

Nevertheless, the old 911 taboos remained; the nagging fear that, pushed too hard in the hands of the unwary, the Porsche would strike like a viper in the bosom. A sense of mistrust? Not quite, but respect is the bedrock of safe progress in any 911, however sophisticated.

FERRARI FRIGHTENER

The Turbo SE was no 935 substitute and nor did it claim to be. Rather, it powerfully combined the challenging character of the 911 Turbo and the svelte chic of the 928S4, and it did it with a mechanical layout as mouthwatering as anything from Modena. The engine was the 3.3-litre all-aluminium

Carrera 4's 3.6-litre flat-six. The best of its breed and good for 250bhp.

Hard-charging 911 Turbo SE – the author attempts to tame the beast.

(Right): *911 Carrera RS 2.7 – when Scotland beckoned, this was the car.*

*Carrera 4 – back to the purity of line that made the 911 famous.
Tail spoiler is concealed and automatically lifts at 50mph for
UK models.*

Rear view of the Carrera RS – this a 1973 example.

flat-six from the regular Turbo but, in the SE, it had acquired a higher-profile camshaft, a bigger turbocharger, a larger charge intercooler and a more efficient exhaust system. Maximum outputs were mighty: 330bhp at 5,750rpm and 318lb ft of torque at 4,000rpm. All this was transmitted to the rear wheels via a four-speed gearbox specially engineered to handle the massive torque. The suspension remained largely unchanged with struts at the front and semitrailing arms at the rear, and anti-roll bars at both ends. The rack and pinion steering went through three turns lock-to-lock.

So the engineering philosophy was unchanged. The Turbo SE, however, looked very different from the regular Turbo. It was still unmistakably a 911 but gone were the characteristic round headlamps, replaced by an entirely new 'flat' nose section with pop-up lights and slim louvres which looked like the gills of a killer shark. Prominent side skirts ran back to the huge flared rear arches which boasted Testarossa-style slats ahead of the rear wheels and admitted air to cool the brakes. The chin spoiler was lower and incorporated a business-like mesh grille, but the rump end had been left alone. It would have been hard to out-do the already huge whale-tail spoiler without being completely reckless.

In line with the ordinary Turbo, the SE got bigger rear wheels and tyres for the 1986 model year. The 225/50 VR 16 tyres on 8in (20cm) rims previously fitted were replaced by gumball 245/45 VR 16s on 9J rims. At the front, 7J×16 wheels shod with 205/55 VR 16 tyres continued to be fitted.

DRIVING MACHINE

The SE also benefited from the 1986 911's improved heating and ventilation system and seats which could be adjusted lower and pushed further back than before. First and last, though, the Turbo SE was a driving machine and a formidable one at that.

The performance was simply devastating with 60mph (96.5kph) coming up in a claimed five seconds and 100mph (160kph) barely more than six seconds later. Flat out meant over 170mph (273kph) or about 10mph (16kph) faster than the standard Turbo. The claim somehow seemed more believable than some.

On the road, the Turbo SE's overtaking ability almost defied belief and this had nothing to do with the very sudden turbo boost characteristics that some fast turbo cars have, and that one relies on to give the necessary kick. With the SE the sensation was that of one long surge towards the horizon with no tricks. Only by unleashing the full fury of the smooth-spinning boxer engine in first and second could the normally well-mannered tail be pushed into a full-blooded slide but lifting off in the wet might easily provoke the same effect when you least wanted it.

Let's be clear about one thing: the SE would out-corner a 911 Carrera any day of the week. In comparative terms, it had a chassis that was both more able and more forgiving though, for sheer chassis feel, the Carrera still had the edge.

SELF CONTROL

The SE's steering was well-weighted and beautifully direct but lacked the fine degree of road surface information the Carreras could convey back to the driver's hands. Grip from the SE's huge, squat tyres was terrific and the tail-heavy chassis' basic desire to understeer did nothing to blunt the initial impression of just how much adhesion there was available. Suspension control ranked with the very best; the ride never felt anything other than firm but neither did it become uncomfortable – the mark of a great chassis. The brakes, as expected, were staggeringly powerful with a firm pedal and reassuringly instant response.

Everything considered, the 911 Turbo SE was a confident statement: next to the 959, as much power, prestige and charisma as you could have sitting behind a Porsche badge. The ultimate 911 this side of £100,000 without question.

PORSCHE 911 CARRERA RS

The Carrera RS was created as an homologation special. All 500 examples of the ini-

911 Turbo 3.3 – blindingly fast but ultimately less rewarding to drive than the best normally-aspirated Carreras.

tial batch were sold within a week of the car's international debut at the 1972 Paris Show. This was the first 911 to bear the Carrera name and, for many, it encapsulated and projected the 911 driving experience more cogently than anything before or since.

The RS was lean and hard-muscled, with no hint of the excess that blunted the cutting edge of some subsequent models. Its 2.7-litre engine developed a solid 210bhp, quite enough to propel the lightweight body (just 2,346lb (1,065kg)) with formidable force. The RS was an object lesson in economy of

purpose – with its appropriately fat tyres and a duck-tailed spoiler it made later models look clumsy.

In fact, 1,800 RS Carreras were made before the Carrera became a regular, and fatter, production model. The high-performance engine, however, was carried over. Its 2,687cc capacity had been achieved by overboring the earlier 2.4 engine and coating the aluminium walls of the cylinders with Nikasil plating to compensate for the loss of the Biral cylinder liners.

The fuel injection for the RS was Bosch's stalwart mechanical system and the com-

911 Turbo SE Cabriolet. More great 911s.

911 Carrera Club Sport.

911 Carrera Club Sport.

911 Turbo SE Cabriolet.

pression ratio a relatively modest 8.5:1 which allowed the use of 91-octane fuel. The 210bhp peak was achieved at a heady 6,300rpm with a less impressive, but still useful, 188lb ft of torque at 5,100rpm. All this was fed to alloy rear wheels wearing, by today's standards, relatively narrow and high-profile 215/60 VR 15 tyres. Those on the front were the slimmer still 185/70s.

WHITE KNIGHT

An overnight stay at a good friend's house in Bedfordshire had given me a fair chance of making Inverness before supper – but much depended on the weather. The simple fact that it was very cold caused concern. The late winter snows which had already brought the south to a virtual standstill were, according to all the forecasts, heading back north. We'd just have to beat them there. If any car had good cause not to get caught by a blizzard, it was the Carrera RS.

Even though the heater – as infuriatingly incomprehensible as ever – hadn't yet infused the chill-box of a cabin with warm air, the car's natural vibrancy was generating its own impression of heat. The slight, tingling vibration from the big flat-six, still to settle to an even beat, massaged the illusion and dissipated potential annoyance with the Porsche's hotch-potch ergonomics, awkward pedal and sticky gearchange.

As we sped through barely stirring villages on our way to the M1, with grey vapour curling out of the small car's drainpipe exhaust, only the trees and hedges wore a crystalline coat; the tarmac looked slightly bleached but was dry and grippy.

Our pedestrian progress past the bus queues and paper delivery boys caused no great interest. Despite its signal blue 'Carrera' side flashes and colour-matched wheel centres, our white Porsche looked much like any other narrow-bodied 911 – compact and disarmingly discreet by supercar standards.

The original-style bumpers, considerably daintier than the sprung impact-absorbing items that gave the 911 a jutting jaw-line from 1974, looked clean and unobtrusive.

After a dozen miles or so, the initially recalcitrant but essentially light and precise gearchange had improved to the point when it no longer required a conscious effort to make it work smoothly. The feeling of intimacy, of 'one-ness' with the car, was growing, too. The last time I'd done this trip had been in a Jaguar XJ 12 almost exactly a year earlier. It was a car which consummately isolated the driver from the action in the manner of most big and heavy cars with super-refined drivetrains, heavily-damped cabins and silent door sealing. The driver was left a sleepy spectator; subdued, curiously uninvolved and unmoved.

THE PLEASUREDOME

The RS could hardly have provided a greater contrast. There was nothing aloof about this car – its contact with the driver was as close as hot breath down a shirt collar; nerve-endings sparked with small but critical inputs, everything etched-out in digital-sharp resolution. The steering, in particular, felt marvellously untainted by compromise damping effects. It jiggled, it kicked, it squirmed – bristling with information. The RS aimed to please absolutely.

I lunched at a favourite pub in the centre of Kendal, the darkly brooding hills of the Lake District in the far distance silhouetted against a flat grey sky. The RS had covered the miles efficiently, comfortably and, above all, enjoyably. Though not without raising many of the old doubts. Whatever else the 911 may have in its favour, it isn't an impregnable dynamic armour.

I'd experienced the normal understeer you get when you point a 911 at a corner and more understeer when I fed in more power. This was annoying. Through the few testing bends this journey had revealed thus far, I'd wanted to get a feel for the RS's point of balance; that narrow band of neutrality just after the understeer stops and before the oversteer begins. I hadn't pushed hard enough. Knowing precisely how hard to push without having to lift-off – that's the key to driving a 911 well and the RS was no different.

I delighted in the motor. There are cars with quieter engines than the 911's flat-six and some are smoother, too. No engine I had ever encountered, however, took such complete control of the hairs on the back of my neck or threatened to plug my spine into the national grid for that *really* tingling sensation. To many, the sound of a current 911's engine in full cry – even corrupted by the muffling veil of a turbo – is music, a subtle mixture of muted induction roar, fan whine and cam drive scream. Though the noise the RS makes is much better. Its note has more leading edge and attack; it is sharp, metallic and raw.

THE ART OF NOISE

As I cranked the engine back into life after lunch, I knew it was a noise I wouldn't tire of. In its anticipation, the afternoon's drive acquired a sense of occasion. It mattered not that the steering wheel obscured many of the instruments, that the ergonomics were a comedy of errors or that the heating and ventilation still did not function properly. None of it mattered when the turn of a key could unleash so much mechanical artistry.

Back on the M6, the RS settled to a brisk yet relaxed 80mph (129kph). Since lunch had taken longer than originally planned, I'd decided that the itinerary would now require only that we reach Loch Lomond by dusk. Much as the Porsche and I might have enjoyed it, there was no need to rush.

We'd reached Carlisle by 4p.m., rush-hour Glasgow by 6p.m. and the Inverbeg Inn on the western shore of Loch Lomond at just after 6.30p.m. This was the place I'd used a year earlier in the Jaguar and, as chance would have it, I was given the same bedroom. We'd packed in just over 350 miles this day. Only another 700 to go.

During the night, warm air arrived on the Gulf stream and rain came with the dawn. Never mind that. It was a morning for miles under wheels along roads which, on the map at least, looked like the tortured death throws of a poisoned serpent.

At Crainlarich I turned on to the A82 and pointed the 911's tightly contoured snout in the direction of Glencoe. The contrast between the RS's eager, nervous responses and the floating indifference of the XJ 12 twelve months earlier as we swept up the hills and swooped into the valleys was nothing short of staggering. The Porsche was eating up the road and, at last, that delicate knife-edge balance which had eluded me the previous day was emerging from the shadow of the understeer. There was so much pure feel, it was hard to think of any other car which would have been as satisfying to drive hard. Doubts that the steering might prove tiring in the long term were unfounded; it had just the right amount of kickback – not a tugging of the rim so much as a gentle writhing, an easy-going action that made a bond between hands and road.

RIDING THE ROLLER-COASTER

If the RS understeered at normal cornering, a brutal bootful of throttle could snap the tail out very suddenly requiring a quick and accurate steering correction. In fact, it was sometimes better to simply ease the grip on the rim and let the steering's strong castor action spin the wheel back and apply its own opposite lock.

Gaining altitude, so the snow we had last seen on the other side of the border returned

Carrera RS 2.7 – a better way to start the day if you have to be in Scotland by teatime.

to bleach out the scenery. What scenery! The mountains now were real rather than big hills and the road swooped between them like the ribbon tail of a stunt kite. The A82, at this point, was quite smooth and its curves constant like a roller-coaster's rather than bumpy and kinked. The RS was feeling better and better, using its scorching mid and upper range acceleration to shrink the straights, powering out of low gear turns with a flick of the tail. This wasn't the cool composure of a BMW or a Mercedes but something that required commitment and concentration from the driver. A momentary lapse might be enough to nudge the whole balancing act over the precipice.

On the part of the A82 that runs from Fort William to the southern edge of Loch Ness, I pushed harder still without really knowing what would happen. The road was a real test for any car punctuated, as it was, with sharp crests, disguised dips and vicious twists. It was the one road that had comprehensively wrong-footed the Jaguar.

In second and third gears, the 911 felt breathtakingly swift between the corners. The more severe bumps, however, were causing problems. Sporadically, the front end would go light and vague, the suspension failing to remove the sting from the severest humps and allowing the body to bob like a cork on a stormy sea. Each time it happened, I was forced to back off – it was impossible to recreate the rhythm and swing that had been so seductive on the smoother roads. I couldn't help thinking that even something as humble as a Peugeot 309 GTi would have sailed on unbowed.

But then the 911 has always demanded

911 TURBO *vs* 928S4 SE		
	911	**928**
cc	3,299	4,957
Max bhp	300	320
Max lb ft	317	317
Max mph	158	160
0–60 secs	4.9	5.5
30–70 secs	4.3	4.7
¼ mile	13.1	13.8
30–50 secs	7.6	4.4
50–70 secs	8.6	6.3
Overall mpg	16.6	18.6
Touring mpg	21.9	20.4
Mph/1,000rpm	27.4	26.1
Weight lb	3,051	3,480

respect from its driver – the RS perhaps more than most. Its smooth-road cornering capabilities can be phenomenal but ultimate suspension control leaves something to be desired. The advice is worth repeating: slow into corners and fast out is the best approach.

Before heading back south, we lunched at Aviemore with blue-nosed skiers in the main hotel. Then it was back to Glasgow and the long haul of endless motorway beyond.

Again, a Porsche 911 had been stimulating company. And the RS wasn't just a great 911 but, I now knew, a great car. With the handful of cassettes I'd brought along for the trip still rattling around in the glovebox, we headed home, the 911 providing the real music of the night.

9 A Slice of the Action

The good news first: 911s were built tough from day one and, despite the fact that just about every aspect of the specification has changed save for the basic mechanical layout, they have become tougher and more durable in the ensuing twenty-seven years. They only remain tough, however, if they haven't been ravaged by rust and, as we shall discover, early 911s aren't just natural victims of the vicious oxide but are prone to severe brutalization.

What is more perplexing to some, however, is that 911s are very different from every other car on the second-hand market (even the VW Beetle has only tenuous genetic ties) and are distanced from casual investigation by a web of buyer-beware intrigue waiting to ensnare the non-expert. Given the root-level desirability of most 911s, it's the notion that the attraction could turn out to be fatal that unsettles the digestion.

Indeed, the very idea of getting financially and emotionally involved with an aspirational purchase that, in the cold light of day, turns out to be a high quality banger has given many would-be 911 owners a severe attack of the jitters — a condition that usually develops into cold feet. This is a shame but an inescapable fact of life. There are too many 911 horror stories for complacency.

A LEAP IN THE DARK

Buying a 911, however, needn't be a nightmare. For the purposes of this chapter, we can rule out cars less than about four years old. Official Porsche dealers root their business in one or two-owner stock and the prices reflect this. Security of mind is high but genuine bargains are virtually non-existent.

The 'non-official' Porsche dealers, on the other hand, can provide a source of more fruitful pickings. These tend to co-operate closely with the Porsche Club of Great Britain, which, with a membership of around 7,500, generates the bulk of their turnover. The symbiosis is cemented by American tyre company and Porsche original equipment suppliers, BF Goodrich who sponsor the club's successful and now well established racing championship. This is where the characters who matter are to be found. Names like Josh Sadler, Bob Watson, Neil Bainbridge and Paul Edwards may not mean much to the uninitiated but, as businessmen who sell, service and race-prepare 911s, they're your best and only friends when the time comes to take that leap in the dark.

Paul Edwards, in particular, is a pivotal player. A successful racer in the Porsche–Goodrich series and an invaluable contact for non-official dealer servicing, Edwards is also a partner in EWP auto parts, a straight-down-the-middle supplier of pattern Porsche parts sourced from proprietary manufacturers. The key here is affordability. Beautifully made and packaged as original Porsche parts undoubtedly are, they don't come cheap. The EWP equivalents are around forty per cent cheaper and have acquired a

METAL DETECTING

So you're not alone: there are people who can give you good advice. However, should you decide to go for broke and search out that once-in-a-lifetime bargain the experts have missed you'll need to arm yourself with some facts that, if you were simply a 911 admirer, *you might prefer to gloss over*. This, in simple terms, is the low-down:

● Not for nothing did Porsche introduce fully galvanised bodyshells in 1976. Beware of the evil rot in 911s made before that date and especially in those that rolled out of Stuttgart before 1971 – they won't even have galvanised floorpans.

● A rotten 911 can cost anything between £7,000 and £10,000 to put right, and that's before you look at the inside.

● Trim parts are very expensive. Buy a 911 with rust *and* an untidy interior and you're in big trouble.

● Targas are generally bad news. The roof panel sealing is a perpetual headache and it's a rare Targa that doesn't creak and groan when it's driven over a bumpy road.

● 911s with the unhappy Sportomatic semi-automatic transmission are to be regarded with suspicion. Definitely an acquired taste, conversion to five-speed manual can cost anything up to £3,000. If it isn't yours though Sportomatics tend to be cheaper in the first place so the cost can be partially offset.

● Avoid 911s that have been obviously interfered with, especially old examples that have been tarted up to look like Turbos or wide-bodied Carreras. Re-builds that disguise accident damage, possibly of insurance 'write-off' proportions, are potentially disastrous – from a safety as well as an investment point of view – so do everything within your power to check histories. As for real Turbos, any example that falls into the 'affordable' category is likely to have problems of a dire nature. When Porsche announced, in 1989, that the Turbo was for the chop, prices went into orbit and, at the time of writing, show little sign of falling back to earth, despite the factory's assurances that a replacement for the Turbo is well underway.

fine reputation in the rebuild trade: they're tough and they do a good job. There . . . no need to re-mortgage the house after all.

ROTTEN LUCK

The chances of being lumbered with a 911 that rapidly reduces itself to a pile of ferrous oxide are greatly reduced, of course, if you know where to look for it while it's still spreading.

The front wings are a good starting point. Wherever there's an accumulation of mud and dirt (the perfect moisture trap) there's likely to be rust: look at the trailing edge of the wing, around the wheelarch lips and around the fuel filler flap. How much rust

The roof panel sealing on the targa top has often been the cause of maintenance problems.

Repair under way on a 911.

you find is largely dependent on how conscientious previous owners were at clearing the debris away. If you find too much, however, the answer could be to replace the wing(s). This isn't as desperate as it sounds since the front wings are bolted on and relatively easy to remove.

Much of the above applies to inspecting the rear wings but, if the worst is found, replacement isn't quite so straightforward because they're welded on. The boxes that house the lights, both front and rear, are also prone to corrosion. These can be bought separately or in-unit with the wing but tend to be expensive.

Perimeter rust is the ominous term applied to sill rot. This is especially serious since the car relies on the inner and outer sills for much of its strength. Expense of replacement isn't the real problem here, but the time and effort required to undertake the job is. And it's a job that simply has to be well done – there's no margin for botched workmanship when the car's structural integrity is at stake.

Targas, which have a weaker bodyshell to start with, can literally sag in the middle if the sills have been attacked by rust (the coupe's strong roof section doesn't allow this to happen but it may not necessarily mean that there isn't a problem).

Rust running along the bottom of doors and the engine lid is common enough but, a morsel of good news for once, the front luggage boot lid usually manages to escape. At the back, though, the panel which supports the number plate is a prime candidate for premature disintegration.

A DEEPER UNDER-STANDING

Not only is the 911's floorpan very strong but surprisingly corrosion resistant. When rust does occur, it's usually around the edges and this can be made good by plating. Weaker spots are the shell's front crossmember and the rear torsion bar tube. The crossmember does an important job: it's the mounting point for the suspension wishbones so a thorough check, especially on pre-C series cars, is essential.

Rear torsion bar maladies are mostly confined to A and B series cars and more insidious because the tube nestles in the depths of the bodyshell. The first sign of weakness is when the tube fails. This is not a subtle effect since it causes the suspension to flop on to the damper mountings. It almost goes without saying that, given the less than forgiving handling characteristics of a 911

The Sportomatic semi-automatic transmission is an acquired taste, but does tend to be cheaper.

in tip-top condition, torsion tube failure is probably the least funny thing that can happen to anyone driving a 911. It's dangerous. You have been warned.

Less dangerous, but more depressing if you discover it too late, is the entry of water into the front of the sill and chassis leg bodywork. This happens when the flange inside the front wing at its trailing edge becomes perforated. The condition is manifested, initially, as sopping wet carpets and, later, as runaway rot. At the back of the car the mild steel oil tanks which nestle inside the rear wings are another target for source rusting and worse. Rusty oil tanks make their own foreign bodies and should one of these migrate to the engine's bearings, the consequences are almost too hideous to con-

template. Stainless steel tanks are the answer.

CHAIN SMOKERS

The 911's apparently immortal flat-six engine is famous for its reliability and longevity but it would be wrong to get the idea that it's maintenance-free. Through long and bitter experience, a generation of 911 owners have pin-pointed the hydraulic timing chain tensioners as the thing that goes wrong most.

Due to the wide span of temperatures they are subjected to by the air-cooled engine, it's rare for them to work efficiently for more than 50,000 miles. Fortunately, the chain makes enough racket when the tensioners are on the way out for the problem to be easily diagnosed and just as easily cured. Neglect, however, can court disaster. Timing chain guides are another potential source of grief. They're usually made of rubber and when they perish oilways become blocked thus starving the camshaft of lubrication.

The average life for valve guides is around 60,000 miles and, once they've had it, you'd better stock up with oil because the engine will become very adept at converting it into smoke. Worn piston rings will add to the oil consumption at around 80,000 miles.

PANDORA'S BOX

Transmission troubles aren't really the domain of the keen do-it-yourselfer but it's as well to know what to look out for. Unsurprisingly, the early gearboxes are most suspect – input shaft weakness with 2-litre cars, intermediate bearing failure with 2 and 2.2-litre cars, leaking oil seals with E and F series cars. Despite the relative ease with which a 911's engine can be removed, transmission work is nearly always expensive because it usually entails the stripping of the gearbox.

To go back to rust. Heat exchangers are

The flat-six may be long-lasting and reliable but it is not maintenance-free.

Rear wings, however, have to be welded on.

A re-sprayed bodyshell.

A 911 in the workshop.

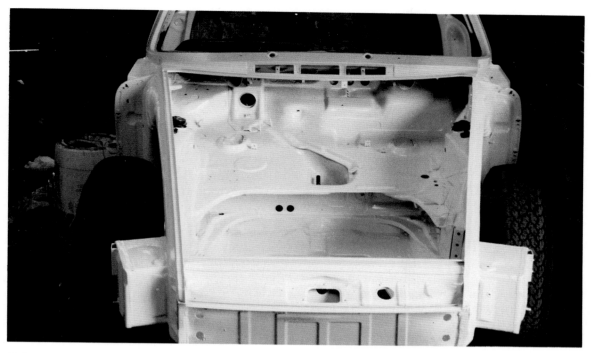

Bolt-on front wings make replacement considerably easier.

Regular servicing is essential if a 911 is going to hold its value long term.

common casualties and, again, it's the big swings in temperature that do the damage: early examples lasted for just two years. Perhaps even more radical than the effect a rotten heat exchanger has on the heater is the effect it has on the wallets of those who own mechanical injection cars. With no supply of heat to know when to turn itself off, the automatic choke simply stays on all the time and drinks petrol.

SEVEN STEPS TO HEAVEN

If any or all of the above makes you want to pack in the whole idea of owning a 911, bear in mind that I haven't even touched on the tales of woe relating to suspension, steering, brakes and even cleverly-concealed accident damage. Naturally, these are areas that have to be investigated (though to be fair, these are reckoned to be less problematical areas).

Worry, by all means, but don't lose sight of the fact you could be buying one of the all-time great sports cars for a very reasonable sum of money. Like so many things, the application of a little time, effort and common sense can work wonders. To finish up, here are a few pointers to help you on your way . . .

1) If the car you want doesn't have an easily verifiable history, don't touch it.

2) If the seller won't agree to an AA or RAC inspection, don't even bother to ask why.

3) View recorded mileages only in the context of overall condition — the old usage versus abusage rule.

4) Don't allow your overall purchase budget to exclude insurance costs. It's no use owning a 911 if you can't afford to drive it.

5) Always go for originals. Back street conversions are bad news, even if they look great.

6) Don't despair if the first 911 you see is a disaster. There are plenty of good ones to choose from.

7) Join the Porsche Club of Great Britain. You'll never be alone.

10 959: The Logical Conclusion?

It is perhaps fitting that the most remarkable sports car of all time should spawn one likely to be remembered as the greatest. That car is the 959, a machine that has carved for itself a place in history as the best and most capable supercar of the 1980s – maybe of the century.

Even before its launch, the 959 had become embroiled in – indeed, was one of the catalysts for – the supercar price controversy that saw the 'value' of Ferraris and limited-run Porsches become locked directly into the greed index of wealthy car collectors. It is a matter of some distress that this phenomenon didn't just hike the resale prices of 'the chosen few' out of the reach of those who might have been able to drive them with an appropriate level of skill and understanding. Instead they went into the hands of those who felt it better not to drive them at all for fear of dislodging one of the zeros from the value.

Ironically, the 959 was the one car that at least some sort of case for a £350,000 price tag could be argued. Here, after all, was a car as good as contemporary technology could make it, an engineering *tour de force* of breathtaking vision and completeness. By comparison, Ferrari's even faster (197mph (317kph) versus 201mph (323kph)) blue chip investment, the F40, looked crude and heavy-handed – freakish muscularity in the presence of genius.

Both cars are beautifully engineered but some argue that neither the 959 nor the F40 can really qualify as 'production cars'; at least the 959 is a practical road car.

WORKING THE FUTURE

Seen by some as a crystal ball, the 959 presented a vision of Porsche's future that has already started to unfold. The eighty-five per cent new Carrera 4, for example, borrows more from the 959 than it does from the 911 and, itself, forms the basis for the extraordinary Panamericana, the best clue yet of which direction the 911 is heading.

Perhaps even more significantly, the 959 is an evocation of a philosophy that has its roots firmly planted in Porsche's distant past. Professor Porsche (and chief engineer Karl Rabe) had a four-wheel drive version of the Beetle on the drawing board even before World War II. Remember, too, that the truly innovative but effectively stillborn mid-engined, four-wheel drive Cisitalia Grand Prix car was one of the Porsche design office's earliest commissions.

It wasn't until the 1980s, however, that Porsche once again turned their attention to four-wheel drive. The story goes that one day a Jensen FF was ushered through the factory gates at Zuffenhausen and, over the ensuing months, was extensively tested and inspected by Porsche's engineers. Nothing much came of this – the company was reported to be unconvinced about the worth of four-wheel drive in a sporting context – but the episode showed that Porsche were keeping all options covered.

As the 1980s beckoned, it was the 911's options that were up for review. Although its termination had been mooted many

959 – not pretty, but what presence.

times before, this time it needed the proverbial shot in the arm to keep it going. No prizes for guessing the medicine. By September 1981 Porsche had an experimental all-drive 911 up and running and, later the same month, the factory displayed a Turbo, four-wheel drive Cabriolet at the Frankfurt Show.

911 LIVES AGAIN

In fact, this was especially encouraging for the old stager since the soft-top element clearly had plenty of commercial mileage and could be used to safeguard the car's immediate future in preparation for the mechanical moves.

Serious development of a four-wheel drive system for production was soon underway and, with it, project 959. Clearly, the new car needed a purpose in life and while this would, as things transpired, include a successful Paris–Dakar rallying career, the 959 was conceived as a Group B racer (with Le Mans very much in mind) and, for this, 200 had to be made.

What Porsche boss Peter Schutz didn't want the 959 to be, however, was just another homologation special. Aesthetically as well as dynamically, the ultimate expression of the 911 would represent the pinnacle of technical achievement with no compromises. This was true enough, but the 959 was also a testbed, allowing a more rapid development of specific 'systems' because it didn't have to conform to normal production constraints or deadlines. Thus it was used for studies on four-wheel drive, chassis, engines, new materials and aerodynamics. If you think the 959's computer-controlled four-wheel drive, six-speed gearbox, Kevlar and aluminium body, two turbochargers and 450bhp sound like the extravagant fantasies of a designer indulging a 'cost-no-object' brief, think again. The 959 had to earn its keep.

Peter Schutz.

That it looks like a 'flattened' 911 is no coincidence. The size, the lightness and the engine of the 911 were important starting points. Part of the 959's technical thrust, however, was to exorcise the compromises inherent in that car's design. yet the 959 is made much like any other 911 – its galvanised steel monocoque uses the same door and window apertures though the floorpan, not surprisingly, is heavily modified to cope with a different set of transmission, engine and suspension requirements. Fully constructed, the monocoque makes a short trip to the Rosslebau factory hall where the real work begins.

ARAMID AVATAR

All the visual changes, with the exception of the bonded windscreen, happen below glass level. The overtly rounded and aerodynamic

A marvel of modern engineering, the 959's twin-turbo 2.8 developed 450bhp at 6,500rpm and powered the car to a top speed of 197mph.

bodywork is fashioned from aramid (a Kevlar derivative). Among the more distinctive aspects of the 959's aesthetic signature are the 944 Turbo-style air ducts low down on the leading edge of the front wheelarches which admit cold air to the water and oil radiators. Headlamps located behind flush, raked glass contribute to the 959's sleeker frontal aspect. A more forceful distortion of the 911's familiar shape are the hugely flared wings, necessary to enclose the 17in (43cm) diameter super-wide tyred magnesium alloy wheels. At the back, the fatter arches work with the integrated aramid

engine cover to provide what is perhaps the 959's best styling trick – the sexy wrap-over rear wing. Given the fact that the 959 is some 10in (25cm) wider than a regular 911, it is little wonder that the new shape has tremendous presence. Not only that, but a Cd (drag factor) of just 0.32 and zero lift at the car's 197mph (317kph) maximum speed.

Originally, the 959's maximum power and weight were quoted at 400bhp and 1,115kg respectively. This was with the intention that 200 examples and twenty evolution cars would be built and homologated by April 1985. In the event, the first 959s weren't delivered to customers until well into 1987 and, by that time, power had risen to 450bhp (430bhp with catalytic converter) and the weight to 1,450kg.

Suspension for the 959 bore little similarity to the 911. Out went the familiar front MacPherson struts and rear torsion bars, replaced by competition-style upper and lower wishbones with dual coil springs and adjustable Bilstein dampers all round. Braking was courtesy of the 962 racer: huge ventilated and cross-drilled discs at each corner with fixed four-piston alloy calipers. Anti-lock was provided by Wabco, a fast-reacting system compatible with four-wheel drive.

Interestingly, Dunlop Denloc tyres – similar to those supplied to the racing team – were originally specified for the 959. These covers would have added to the impressive level of emergency safety already provided by the Bosch/Porsche pressure-loss warning system by having locked beads to keep them on the rim even when deflated. But at a late stage, Dunlop failed to homologate the Denloc for road use and Porsche switched to the still excellent Bridgestone RE71 unidirectional rubber.

A TAIL OF TWO TURBOS

Such meticulous attention to detail at the business end of the 959's chassis was, of course, essential with the performance potential of this Porsche's engine – at the time, the most powerful ever offered in a production road car, developing 450bhp at 6,500rpm and 369lb ft of torque at 5,500rpm.

The 2.8-litre twin-turbo flat-six is derived from the 956/962 racing unit with water-cooled four-valve-per-cylinder heads for each air-cooled bank. Unusually, for such a potent engine, the valves are hydraulically actuated via inverted cup tappets. In spite of this, the rev limit is set at 8,000rpm with the

engine 'safe' to 8,500rpm, though the polished titanium connecting rods undoubtedly help here.

The twin KKK turbos have their own intercoolers and blow into a common plenum chamber, but not always at the same time. The primary turbo starts to build boost pressure from around 1,200rpm, hitting a peak of 1 bar (14psi). Up to this point, the secondary turbo is passive, a non-return valve isolating it from system boost. It gets its chance to join in from 4,000rpm, raising the overall boost pressure to 2bar (28psi) in hard driving. An electronically-controlled wastegate limits the maximum boost pressure and dictates a minimum level at part throttle, thus reducing exhaust back-pressure and maintaining good efficiency.

Just as exciting as the 959's engine, however, is its six-speed manual transmission which directs power – via a racing-type hydraulically-operated, sintered clutch – to all four wheels in quantities that vary according to the directions of an electronic 'black box' which controls two torque-splitting multi-plate clutches. The simpler of these nestles between the back wheels while the PSK (Porsche Control Clutch) sees service on the front of the rear transaxle. The system offers a greater span of control than would be possible with mechanical or viscous coupling systems. What's more, the driver can partially override the 'black box' control should he anticipate an icy surface ahead.

In fact, the transmission allows the driver to choose from four modes. These are for 'normal' dry road conditions, 'wet' surfaces and 'snow and ice'. Finally, there is also a 'traction' facility which physically locks the clutch for a 50:50 split when the going gets really slippery. What the different modes do, in effect, is decide how much understeer to dial in. And they do it by taking account of the dynamic weight distribution as well as wheel slip. When stationary, the 959 has a 40:60 weight bias but, with hard accelera-

*Much of the 959's body is made from aramid – a member of the
Kevlar family – which clothes a galvanised steel monocoque.*

959 cabin – still unmistakably 911.

959's dramatic front spoiler scoops channel air towards the brakes for cooling.

959 engine in situ.

The 1984 Group B design study that eventually became the 959.
Note the relative lack of scoops and ducts.

959's mighty flat-six in component form.

A real corridor of power.

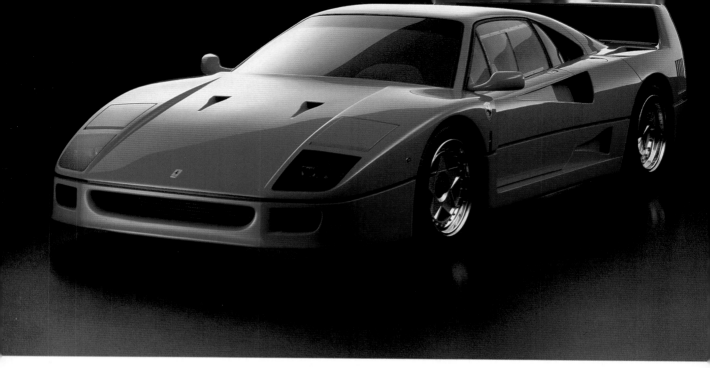

(Above): *Ferrari's fabulous F40: the only production car in existence with a higher top speed than the 959's 197mph – albeit by just 4mph.*

(Below): *959 engines await installation.*

tion, up to eighty per cent of the weight transfers to the rear wheels. The torque split span therefore ranges between 20:80 with the front clutch plates almost fully apart to 50:50 with them completely locked.

At least that's how it is with the 'Confort' version of the 959. The 'Sport' version comes with a special microchip and gives a more sporting 35:65 split as the datum point. Oversteer is possible in this car.

NEW SUSPENSION

Let's not forget the suspension in all of this. The upper and lower arms are designed for minimum camber change with the very wide wheels and tyres (8in (20cm) and 235/45 front, 9in (22cm) and 255/40 rear) and one of each pair of the dual dampers fitted all round is electronically controlled. These firm up at speed irrespective of the manual setting. Likewise, there are three ride-height settings – 120, 150 and 180mm – with automatic override that selects the lowest setting when the car is travelling at speed (greater than 100mph (160kph)). Left to its own devices, the ride management system selects the lowest setting as the 'normal setting'.

The hydraulic system interconnecting the dampers removes the need for anti-roll bars since a small mercury switch detects accelerations in any direction and stiffens up whichever damper is under load. A more conventional application of hydraulics is the 959's power steering – deemed necessary by Porsche's engineers because of the natural conflict between very wide front tyres and suitably direct gearing. It's been possible to retain the 911's standard ratio of 18.2:1 but in an effort to preserve as much of that car's famous feedback as possible, the rack is made from a polished, hard-chrome material.

ENTER THE CARRERA 4

The decision to build a more affordable all-drive 911 was taken on 23 March 1984. The prototype was called 964. By that time the 959 project was already well advanced, which meant that the new car could feed off the experience already gained.

The 964 couldn't take the design liberties the 959 had. It couldn't, for instance, make do with the smaller rear seats – necessary, in the 959's case, to accommodate the six-speed transmission. Nor could it really afford to sacrifice luggage space under the front bonnet, despite the space that would inevitably be taken up by a new, driven front axle.

There were to be other differences, too. The 959's sophisticated PSK torque-apportioning system would remain the exclusive preserve of the 'ultimate 911'. The 964 would, instead, have a centre differential with central lock-up. Not the Torsen differential favoured by Audi, though. Porsche had decided, at an early stage, that, along with most viscous couplings, it simply wasn't strong enough for the job. The research was nothing if not thorough. Even a freewheel in the front drive was tried but, in the end, more energy was devoted to finding the correct torque-split using planetary centre differentials. The extremes were 30:70 and 40:60, based on a static weight distribution of 42:58.

In the end, the system was finalised with a basic split of 31:69, but with the ability to vary automatically to the extremes of either 100 per cent front drive or 100 per cent rear drive.

The Carrera 4 was on its way.

11 The Supercar That Won't Die

The Carrera 4 went on sale in the autumn of 1988 and, against a background of falling profits, it was not a moment too soon. Clearly, the 911 would only survive and prosper if Porsche did the same and the company's performance for 1988 gave little cause for optimism at Zuffenhausen.

At the root of Porsche's problems was an over-reliance on the American market at the time of a falling dollar exchange rate. The situation wasn't helped by what was already being recognised as the burden of sustaining three model ranges – 944, 928 and 911. 'It must be our aim to plan for a future in which we shall use two basic types to concentrate entirely on the exclusive and expensive end of the market', said Ferry Porsche.

In the 1987/1988 business year, the share of vehicles exported to the United States dropped from sixty-five to less than forty per cent, and in the first six months of 1989, sales fell from 8,806 to 4,556 units. The news was bad enough for newly appointed chairman Heinz Branitzky to concede: 'This is undoubtedly the most difficult year we have ever had in America'. However, he did add: 'The worst is behind us'.

What lies ahead for Porsche, of course, depends very much on the Carrera 4 and its rear drive running mate the Carrera 2. The early orders for these cars suggest that they could turn the tide. And it wouldn't be the first time that the 911 has provided a lifeline for its maker.

The first performance test of the Carrera 4 to appear in a British magazine is reprinted at the end of this chapter courtesy of *Autocar & Motor*. Meanwhile, for the 1990 model year, it's the Carrera 2 on which much will depend and this chapter also incorporates a test of that car. Available as a coupe, targa and cabriolet, it's already being hailed as 'the purist's Porsche'.

Powered by the same normally-aspirated 250bhp 3.6-litre boxer engine as its all-drive stablemate, the Carrera comes with ABS anti-lock braking, power-assisted steering, a catalytic converter, a ten-speaker stereo and

---

911 CARRERA 2

Body: Two-door coupe-targa bodywork, electrically-extended rear spoiler.

Engine: Air-cooled, six-cylinder, four-stroke, boxer engine, dry-sump lubrication, three-way catalytic converter.

Bore	100mm
Stroke	76.4mm
Displacement	3,600cc
Compression	11.3:1
Output	250bhp/6,100rpm
Max torque	229lb dt/4,800rpm

Driveline: Engine and gearbox bolted into single drive unit in the rear, hydraulic, dual-circuit brake system with four vented discs, servo and ABS.

Weights

Empty	1,350kg
Total	1,690kg

Claimed performance:
Acceleration from 0–100kph (62mph) in 5.7secs, top speed 162mph

*Front and rear shots of the Porsche 911 Carrera 4
Cabriolet at the 1989 Motor Show.*

the promise of performance that was previously the preserve of the discontinued 911
Turbo. Porsche believes that the Carrera 2
represents 'the new 911 era' and is a worthy
successor to all previous guardians of the
'Carrera' name.

Perhaps the most exciting and significant
feature of the Carrera 2, however, is the
option to provide the 'Tiptronic' dual-
function transmission. This is the first not
wholly manual gearbox offered on a 911
since the ill-starred 'Sportomatic'. The so-
called dual functionality of the new gearbox
is achieved by combining elements of the
PDK twin-clutch transmission (of 962 C
racer fame) with a conventional torque converter.

The lever can move in two gates. One is
marked out with the familiar 1–2–3–D–R
–P automatic pattern, the other has just two

positions, '+' and '−' for manual up and
down shifts. The PDK system ensures that
the engine always remains in harness –
there are no de-clutching pauses in the
power flow. The inevitable electronic 'black
box' control means that there's no danger of
over-revving, either. Electronics also provide an 'intelligent' shift program which
avoids undesirable upshifts before or in a
corner. It works by monitoring driving conditions via the throttle position and reading
lateral g-force during cornering. The driver
can alternate between the two modes as he
pleases and starts are possible in both lever
positions.

Further down the road, there are more
developments for the 911 but, unfortunately,
the much-rumoured 965 – the 'poor man's'
959 – won't be one of them. The project has
been killed-off, a result of soaring develop-

ment costs and too many hitches with the 24-valve boxer engine that would have powered it. There will, however, be a new 911 Turbo. The word is that it will retain the previous model's 2-valve-per-cylinder 3.3-litre engine but will look like a wide-bodied Carrera 2. Even with the catalyst, it will develop around 330bhp and should have a top speed in the region of 170mph (273kph). A Carrera 2 Speedster and six-speed manual gearbox are also on the cards.

The next generation of boxer engines are believed to be water-cooled multi-valve designs and won't just be confined to the 911. A flat-six might easily see its way into the 944 and a flat-eight (maybe even a flat-twelve) into whatever replaces the 928. The future route for the 911, however, seems clear enough. rear engine, rear-wheel drive and four-wheel drive. What the next 911 may look like, few commentators would care to guess, though the extraordinary Panamericana styling exercise hints at one direction.

Just take a long hard look at the Carrera 4. It's an honest shape, resulting from a skilful purification of one that millions have loved. The people at Porsche know how precious the 911 is. They're unlikely to risk the venture now.

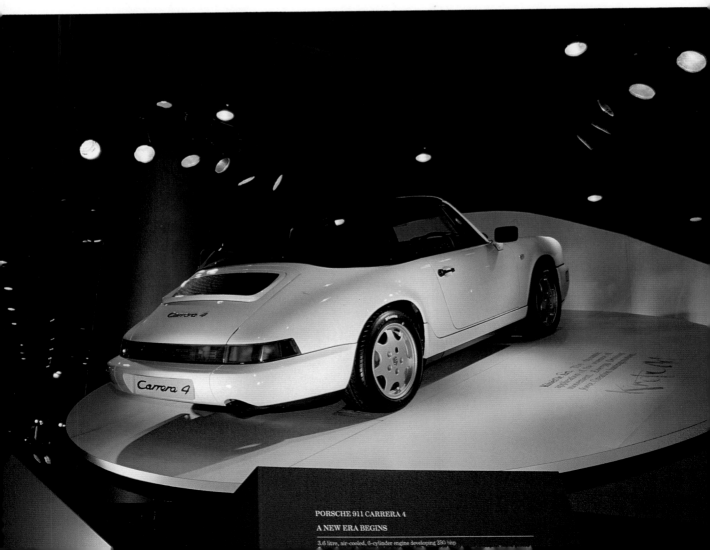

PORSCHE 911 CARRERA 4
A NEW ERA BEGINS
3.6 litre, air-cooled, 6-cylinder engine developing 250 bhp

The Porsche 911 Speedster.

911: THE PRODUCTION STORY

1963

901

1,991cc. 80/66mm bore/stroke. 9.0:1 cr. 130bhp.
Remarks
Presented at the Frankfurt Motor Show as successor to the 356, the 911 (née 901) continued the basic concept of air-cooled boxer engine in the rear of the car. There are big differences nevertheless: larger cabin and boot, new torsion bar suspension, 'safety' steering, MacPherson strut suspension at front, semi-trailing arms at the back, increased performance from six-cylinder engine.

1965–1967

911 2.0

1,991cc. 80/66mm bore/stroke. 9.0:1 cr. 130bhp. 10,723 units produced.
Remarks
901 becomes 911 in the market place because of Peugeot's protest. Rim width is 4.5in (11cm) (the same as 356 C), wiper arms park to the right, 911 script is slanted to the right. Engine breathes through six Solex carburettors; power drives to rear wheels via five-speed gearbox. Side mirrors are round in shape. As of 1967 model year, Targa removable roof panel option with roll-over bar, folding rear window with zipper and Weber carburettors.

1965–1969

912

1,582cc. 82.5/74mm bore/stroke. 9.3:1 cr. 90bhp. 30,300 units produced.
Remarks
Economy version of 911 with simplified trim and 1.6-litre, flat-four engine from 356 C, but reduced from 95 to 90bhp to improve flexibility. Top speed was 112mph (180kph). A car of humble aspirations but a sales success nevertheless. Targa version introduced in 1967.

1967–1969

911S 2.0 Coupe/
Targa

1,991cc. 80/66mm bore/stroke. 9.8:1 cr. 160bhp. 5,056 units produced.
Remarks
As 911 except for: forged pistons, larger valves, two Weber triple-choke carburettors, forged light alloy rims (Fuchs).

As of 1968 model year:

Optional semi-automatic Sportomatic gearbox, 5.5in (14cm) rims, black-finish wipers, rubber bumper inserts.

As of 1969 model year:

Mechanical manifold fuel injection, 170bhp, oil cooler in right front wing. Alternator up-rated to 770 watts, halogen headlights introduced. Wheelbase lengthened to 2,268mm, rims widened to 6in (15cm). Targa gets fixed window with ventilation slits in the roll bar. Three-stage heating and ventilation system. Disc brakes all round; anti-roll bars front and rear.

1968–1969

911T 2.0 Coupe/
Targa

1,991cc. 80/66mm bore/stroke. 8.6:1 cr. 110bhp. 6,318 units produced.
Remarks
Replacement for the 911 incorporating 912 chassis layout and trim. The 'T' stood for Touring. Four-speed gearbox standard.

As of 1969 model year:

Five-speed gearbox.

1969

911L 2.0 Coupe/Targa

1,991cc. 80/66mm bore/stroke. 9.0:1 cr. 130bhp. 11,610 units produced.
Remarks
Mechanically similar to discontinued base 911 with 911S-style trim. Four or five-speed gearbox. Semi-auto Sportomatic optional.

1969

911E 2.0 Coupe/Targa

1,991cc. 80/66mm bore/stroke. 9.1:1 cr. 140bhp. 2,826 units produced.
Remarks
Superseded 911L and largely similar to 911S. Mechanical manifold injection, hydro-pneumatic self-levelling rear axle option.

1970–1971

911T 2.2 Coupe/Targa

2,195cc. 84/66mm bore/stroke. 8.6:1 cr. 125bhp. 15,082 units produced.
Remarks
Further development of 911T becomes most popular model. Ventilated all-disc braking, two triple-choke downdraught carburettors, four-speed gearbox standard with Sportomatic option.

911E 2.2 Coupe/Targa

2,195cc. 84/66mm bore/stroke. 9.1:1 cr. 155bhp. 4,927 units produced.
Remarks
Bigger-engined replacement for 911E with trim from S. Four or five-speed gearbox, Sportomatic optional.

911S 2.2 Coupe/Targa

2,195cc 84/66mm bore/stroke. 9.8:1 cr. 180bhp. 4,691 units produced.
Remarks
More power and torque for S. Large intake and exhaust passages for cylinder head, five-speed gearbox and optional limited slip differential but no Sportomatic. US version gets tank vent and alarm system.

1972–1973

911T 2.4 Coupe/Targa

2,341cc. 84/70.4mm bore/stroke. 7.5:1 cr. 130bhp. 16,933 units produced.
Remarks
First of the third generation cars. Low compression ratio means regular grade fuel can be used. New four-speed manual gearbox (optional five-speed or Sportomatic), two triple-choke downdraught carburettors, oil filter under lid on right side of body near B-pillar, smooth front bumpers. US version gets fuel injection, 140bhp. 1973 model year: black trim, rectangular exterior mirror, 2,271mm wheelbase, stainless steel exhaust. US version gets optional Bosch K-Jetronic fuel injection.

911E 2.4 Coupe/Targa

2,341cc. 84/70.4mm bore/stroke. 8.1:1
Remarks
More muscular version of T, but with same basic equipment. Runs on regular grade fuel but has fuel injection. Painted 6in (15cm) steel rims standard.

For 1973 model year: 911S-style front spoiler.

Porsche 911 Carrera 2 at the 1989 Motor Show.

Carrera 2 Cabriolet for model year 1990.

911S 2.4 Coupe/ Targa	2,341cc. 84/70.4mm bore/stroke. 8.5:1 cr. 190bhp. 5,094 units produced.
	Remarks
	More potent edition of E, but with some basic equipment. Fuel injection but runs on regular grade fuel. Top speed 143mph (230kph). 6in (15cm) light alloy rims and front spoiler standard.

1973

911 Carrera RS 2.7 Coupe	2,387cc. 90/70.4mm bore/stroke. 8.5:1 cr. 210bhp. 1,590 units produced.
	Remarks
	Further development of the 911S 2.4. First 911 to use Carrera name. Three versions: Sport, Touring and Race. Widened rear wings, 6in (15cm) front rims, 7in (18cm) rear rims. Rear 'ducktail' spoiler and deeper front spoiler. Stainless steel exhaust system, Carrera script and rims available in three colours: red, blue and green. Major sporting successes on world's race tracks.

1974

911 Carrera RS 3.0 Coupe	2,993cc 95/70.4mm bore/stroke. 9.8:1 cr. 230bhp. 109 units produced.
	Remarks
	Replaces the 911 Carrera RS 2.7. Carrera RS 3.0 was sold for DM65,000 (around £20,300): fifty cars are converted to RSR 3.0 specification for race and rally use.

1974–1977

911 2.7 Coupe/ Targa	2,687cc. 90/70.4mm bore/stroke. 8.0:1 cr. 150bhp. 17,260 units produced.
	Remarks
	Traditional 'T' and 'E' designations are dropped. Bumpers incorporate 'accordion-bellows' style impact dampers, 'safety' steering wheel, seats with integral head restraints, K-Jetronic injection, four-speed gearbox, mechanical clutch aid, seat belts, 80-litre (17.6-gallon) fuel tank.
For 1975 model year:	Modified heat exchanger, 980 watt alternator, 6in (15cm) clutch, light-alloy rims.
For 1976 model year:	165bhp, five-blade cooling fan, automatic cold start system, electrically adjusted and heated exterior mirror. Galvanized body with 6-year anti-rust guarantee.
911S 2.7 Coupe/ Targa	2,687cc. 90/70.4mm bore/stroke. 8.5:1 cr. 175bhp. 17,124 units produced.
	Remarks
	High performance derivative of 2.7 with same basic equipment.
For 1976 model year:	S only available in the USA, with 165bhp.

1974–1975

911 Carrera 2.7 Coupe/Targa

2,687cc. 90/70.4mm bore/stroke. 8.5:1 cr. 210bhp. 3,353 units produced.
Remarks
Adopted by production programme thanks to sales success of limited-run original 911 Carrera RS 2.7. Basic equipment as for 911 2.7 but with mechanical fuel injection, electric window lifters, exterior mirror and headlight trim painted body colour. Certain markets get Turbo-style rear spoiler, black trim parts, leather-rimmed steering wheel, 6/7in (15/18cm) light-alloy rims (Fuchs), widened rear wings.

For 1975 model year:

Headlight cleaning system standard.

1975–1977

911 Turbo 3.0 Coupe

2,994cc. 95/70.4mm bore/stroke. 6.5:1 cr. 260bhp. 2,173 units produced.
Remarks
First production sports car in the world with turbocharger. Sets new standards for 911 performance. High levels of equipment and trim. Breakerless HKZ ignition system, 7J×14 front rims, 8J×15 rear rims, wide-body shell, large front spoiler, flat rear spoiler. New, stronger four-speed gearbox. Three-spoke steering wheel.

For 1977 model year:

16in (40cm) diameter rims with ultra-low profile tyres, brake servo, assisted clutch.

1975

912E Coupe

1,971cc. 94/71.1mm bore/stroke. 7.6:1 cr. 90bhp. 2,092 units produced.
Remarks
912 makes a brief comeback some six years after it was dropped. Made exclusively for export markets. Two-litre flat-four engine has electronic fuel injection from Type 914-4.

1976–1977

911 Carrera 3.0 Coupe/Targa

2,994cc 95/70.4mm bore/stroke. 8.5:1 cr. 200bhp. 3,691 units produced.
Remarks
Replacements for 911 Carrera 2.7. Basic equipment as for predecessor but with Bosch K-Jetronic injection, five-speed gearbox (four-speed or Sportomatic optional).

For 1977 model year:

All three gearbox variations, brake servo and automatic heater regulation standard.

1978–1983

911SC Coupe/ Targa

2,994cc. 94/70.4mm bore/stroke. 8.5:1 cr. 180bhp. 57,972 units produced.
Remarks
SC supersedes both 911 2.7 and Carrera 3.0. Output originally 180bhp. Basic equipment as for predecessors but with 11-blade cooling fan, fixed rear side windows, 6J×15 front rims, 7J×15 rear rims (16in (40cm)) diameter rims optional).

The author driving the 1989 Speedster.

Impressions of the 965, the 'poor man's' 959 that was shelved.

Porsche Panamericana. A serious interpretation of tomorrow's 911? It seems not.

For 1980 model year:	Output increased to 188bhp (cr 8.6:1).
For 1981 model year:	Output increased to 204bhp (cr 9.8:1).
For 1982 model year:	Cabriolet model introduced.

1978

911 Turbo 3.3

3,299cc. 97/74.4mm bore/stroke. 7.0:1 cr. 300bhp. 15,196 units produced.

Remarks
Development of 911 Turbo with still more power and performance. Turbocharger gets intercooler this time. Basic equipment up-dated to 911 Carrera (3.2)-spec as of 1984 but with bigger rear spoiler, four-speed gearbox, 7in (18cm) front rims, 9in (23cm) rear rims.

For 1980 model year:	Dual exhaust pipes.
For 1985 model year:	Four-spoke steering wheel.
For 1986 model year:	Cabriolet and Targa variants.
For 1989 model year:	Five-speed gearbox. Production discontinued mid-1989.

1984

911 Carrera 3.2 Coupe/Targa/ Cabriolet

3,164cc. 95/74.4mm bore/stroke. 10.3:1 cr. 231bhp. 62,638 units produced.

Remarks
Replacement for 911SC. New: fully-electronic fuel injection and programmed ignition (Motronic), overrun fuel cut-off, fog lights integrated into front skirt, 'Carrera' script on tail. Optional nose and tail spoilers and 'Turbo-look' coupe.

For 1985 model year:	Electrically adjusted seats, optional 'Turbo-look' for Cabriolet and Targa.
For 1986 model year:	'Carrera cat' with 217bhp.
For 1987 model year:	Hydraulically-activated clutch, new five-speed gearbox.

1987

959 Coupe

2,848cc. 95/67mm bore/stroke. 8.3:1 cr. 450bhp. 200 units produced.

Remarks
The ultimate 911 derivative and a development testbed for future Porsche products. Production run limited to 200 units. Water-cooled four-valve heads on air-cooled cylinders, two turbochargers with staged boost, polished titanium rods, forged cylinder heads, hydraulic valve adjustment. All-wheel drive with electronically-controlled power split. Speed-dependant ride height system.

ROAD TEST
Porsche 911 Carrera 2

Reproduced from *Autocar & Motor*
6 December 1989

Questions. The Porsche Carrera 2 poses more than perhaps any other model in the 911's illustrious 26-year history. Is this, the new staple 911, better than the £6000 pricier all-drive Carrera 4? Is it a worthy successor to the thrill-raw Carrera 3.2 it effectively replaces. Is it good enough to take Porsche profitably into the '90s? Is it, indeed, the best 911 yet?

*The early indications suggest that it is all of these things. In a recent showdown with its all-drive running mate (*Autocar & Motor* 1 November), the Carrera 2 won by a short head, providing even greater driver rewards than the fabulous 4 on demanding German roads. Here, in the UK's first full road test, we probe deeper still.*

Already the Carrera 2 has a formidable reputation to live up to. It's the one well-heeled 911 purists are clamouring for, cheque books flapping in the rush. With the delivery of the first right-hand-drive models, though, some doubts have even now been expressed – mostly concerning ride quality and harshness. We can confirm that they're well founded, more on which later. Thankfully, the rest of the news is almost exclusively good.

Perhaps best of all is the Carrera 2's price of £41,505. It's faintly ludicrous to talk of bargain material in the rarefied air of supercar pricing structures, but there's no denying that the Porsche is very competitively pitched. Even Lotus's stunningly well-evolved but still plastic and four-cylinder Esprit Turbo SE costs £1000 more and Ferrari's delectable but less accelerative 348 is a whole BMW 535i more at £64,503.

In essence, the Carrera 2 is a Carrera 4 with two-wheel drive and, like the 4, avail-

able in coupe, targa and cabriolet forms. There are no visual differences externally, save for the (delete option) badging and only 'spot-the-difference' clues on the inside. Both are strongly reminiscent of previous 911s, too, though the intended back-to-basic purity of the new smoothed-off design – concealing 85 per cent fresh hardware beneath – hasn't met with universal praise.

Some feel that the wraparound bumpers look a touch heavy-handed and that the self-raising tail spoiler, while purely functional, does little to enhance the Carrera 2/4's styling on the move. Others are adamant that the new car must be counted among the best looking 911s to date. Perhaps the most important thing is the reduction of the drag coefficient from the 0.395 of the old-style 911 to 0.32.

For the 2, the rear wheels are driven by the same tail-slung injected 3.6-litre flat-six engine and via an only slightly modified version of the 4's excellent five-speed manual gearbox. Thanks to new cylinder heads, pistons, conrods and crankshaft – as well as dual ignition using twin plugs per cylinder – the latest edition of the naturally-aspirated boxer unit is also the most powerful, developing its 250bhp at 6100rpm and 228lb ft at 4800rpm. A three-way catalytic converter is standard kit, as with the C4.

Also shared with the 4 are power-assisted rack and pinion steering and identical negative offset suspension geometry at the front while at the rear the inner semi-trailing arms provide a toe-in correction to improve stability in cornering. Wheels and tyres are the same, too: elegant seven-spoke alloys shod with 205/55VR 16s at the front and 225/50ZR 16s at the rear (Bridgestone RE71s on our test car).

Performance and Economy
A top speed of 158mph is slightly better than the Carrera 4's 156mph – almost certainly a function of energy lost through the all-drive car's transmission – and all but ties with the

New Carrera has cleanest 911 shape for decades though some think bumpers are heavy-handed.

*Front seats are excellent, driving position less good.
Rear seats convert into luggage platform.*

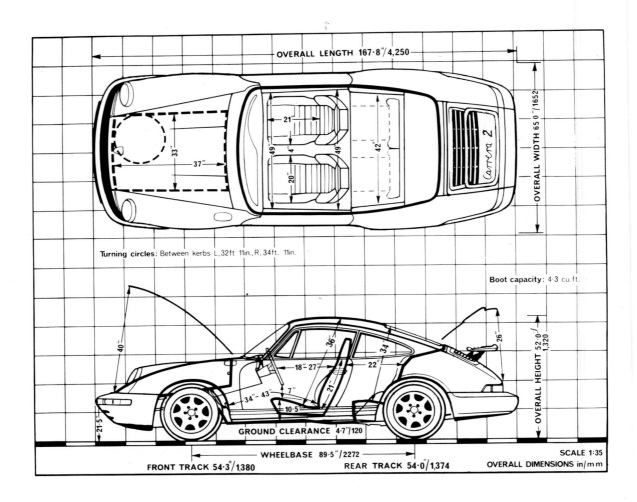

OVERALL LENGTH 167·8″/4,250

OVERALL WIDTH 65 0″/1652

Carrera 2

Turning circles: Between kerbs L,32ft 11in.,R,34ft. 11in.

Boot capacity: 4·3 cu.ft.

OVERALL HEIGHT 52·0″/1,320

GROUND CLEARANCE 4·7″/120

WHEELBASE 89·5″/2272

FRONT TRACK 54·3″/1,380   REAR TRACK 54·0″/1,374

SCALE 1:35
OVERALL DIMENSIONS in/mm

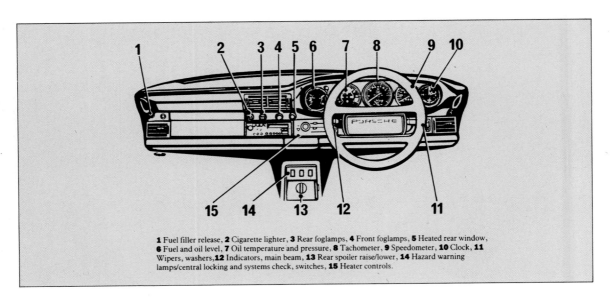

1 Fuel filler release, **2** Cigarette lighter, **3** Rear foglamps, **4** Front foglamps, **5** Heated rear window, **6** Fuel and oil level, **7** Oil temperature and pressure, **8** Tachometer, **9** Speedometer, **10** Clock, **11** Wipers, washers, **12** Indicators, main beam, **13** Rear spoiler raise/lower, **14** Hazard warning lamps/central locking and systems check, switches, **15** Heater controls.

SPECIFICATION

ENGINE
Longitudinal, rear-wheel drive.
Capacity 3600cc, 6 cylinders horizontally opposed.
Bore 100mm, **stroke** 76.4mm.
Compression ratio 11.3 to 1.
Head/block Light alloy/light alloy.
Valve gear dohc, 2 valves per cylinder.
Ignition and fuel Electronic twin ignition. Bosche L-Jetronic DME controlled fuel injection.
Max power 250bhp (PS-DIN) (184kW ISO) at 6100rpm. **Max torque** 228lb ft (310 Nm) at 4800rpm.

TRANSMISSION
5-speed manual.

Gear	Ratio	mph/1000rpm
Top	0.868	24.2
4th	1.086	19.3
3rd	1.407	14.9
2nd	2.059	10.2
1st	3.500	6.0

Final drive ratio 3.44 to 1.

SUSPENSION
Front, independent, struts, lower wishbones, coil springs, telescopic dampers, anti-roll bar.
Rear, independent, semi-trailing arms, coil springs, telescopic dampers, anti-roll bar.

STEERING
Rack and pinion, power assisted, 2.9 turns lock to lock.

BRAKES
Front 11.8ins (298mm) dia ventilated discs.
Rear 11.8ins (298mm) dia discs.

WHEELS/TYRES
Light alloy, 6ins rims (front).
8ins rims (rear). 205/55ZR16 front/225/50ZR17 rear tyres.

COSTS

Prices
Total (in UK)	£41,505
Delivery, road tax, plates	£161
On the road price	£41,666
Total as tested	£41,505

SERVICE
Major service 12,000 miles – service time 8.5hrs.

PARTS COST (Inc VAT)
Oil filter	£8.97
Air filter	£10.95
Spark plugs (set)	£20.88
Brake pads (2 wheels) front	£83.99
Brake pads (2 wheels) rear	£31.99
Exhaust complete*	£510.09
Windscreen	£216.94
Headlamp unit	£98.54
Front wing	£312.16
Rear bumper	£231.26

* Inc. catalytic converter

WARRANTY
24 months/unlimited mileage, 10 years anti-corrosion, 10 years against paint defects, 24 months breakdown recovery

EQUIPMENT
Anti-lock brakes	●
Central locking	●
Alloy wheels	●
Auto gearbox	TBA
Power assisted steering	●
Limited slip differential	£741
Steering rake/reach adjustment	●
Seat height adjustment	●
Electric seat adjustment	£422
Lumbar adjustment	●
Head restraints	●
Intermittent wipe	●
Heated seats	£197
Leather trim	£1142
Air conditioning	£1944
Cruise control	£374
Radio/cassette player	●
Electric aerial	●
8 Speakers	●
Electric windows	●
Internal headlamp adjustment	●
Front fog/driving lamps	●
Headlamp wash wipe	●
Electric tilt/slide sunroof	£1245
Metallic paint	£847

● Standard – Not available TBA To be announced

PERFORMANCE

MAXIMUM SPEEDS
Gear	mph	km/h	rpm
Top (Mean)	158	254	6529
(Best)	160	257	6611
4th	135	217	7000
3rd	104	167	7000
2nd	71	114	7000
1st	42	67	7000

ACCELERATION FROM REST
True mph	Time (secs)	Speedo mph
30	2.1	32
40	3.0	44
50	4.0	55
60	5.1	67
70	6.7	78
80	8.3	89
90	10.2	100
100	12.7	111
110	15.3	121
120	18.7	131
130	23.7	142

Standing ¼-mile: 13.6secs, 104mph
Standing km: 24.6secs, 132mph
30–70mph thro' gears 4.6secs

SOLD IN UK BY
Porsche Cars Great Britain Limited
Bath Road
Calcot, Reading, Berks RG3 7SE
Telephone 0734 303666

ACCELERATION IN EACH GEAR
mph	Top	4th	3rd	2nd
10–30	–	–	4.7	2.9
20–40	8.2	5.7	4.1	2.7
30–50	7.5	5.4	4.0	2.4
40–60	7.3	5.4	4.0	2.3
50–70	7.4	5.5	3.6	–
60–80	7.6	5.3	3.3	–
70–90	8.1	5.0	3.5	–
80–100	8.1	5.1	–	–
90–110	7.7	5.3	–	–
100–120	8.2	6.0	–	–
110–130	8.2	–	–	–
120–140	11.3	–	–	–

FUEL CONSUMPTION
Overall mpg: 20.4 (13.8 litres/100km)
Touring mpg*: 26.4mpg (11.5 litres/100km)
Govt tests mpg: 16.5mpg (urban)
36.2mpg (56mph)
29.1mpg (75mph)
Grade of fuel: Unleaded (95RM) or (98+ RM)
Tank capacity: 16.9 galls (77 litres)
Max range*: 416 miles
* Based on Government fuel economy figures: 50 per cent of urban cycle, 25 per cent each of 56/75mph consumptions.

BRAKING
Fade (from 104mph in neutral)
Pedal load (lb) for 0.5g stops

	start/end		start/end
1	35–35	6	55–40
2	45–45	7	55–40
3	40–35	8	55–40
4	45–40	9	55–35
5	45–40	10	55–30

Response (from 30mph in neutral)
Load	g	Distance
10lb	0.12	250ft
20lb	0.38	79ft
30lb	0.63	48ft
40lb	0.90	33ft
50lb	1.10	27ft

WEIGHT
Kerb 3040lb/1380kg
Distribution % F/R 36/64
Test 3326lb/1510kg
Max towing weight 6365lb/2890kg

TEST CONDITIONS
Wind	7–14mph
Temperature	9deg C (48deg F)
Barometer	1016mbar
Surface	dry asphalt
Test distance	943 miles

Figures taken at 2707 miles by our own staff at the Lotus Group proving ground, Millbrook.

Carrera 2 can be breathtakingly rapid on twisty roads but uncomfortable, too. Suspension is firm to the point of harshness. Bump-thump is severe.

250 bhp flat-six is best yet.

As familiar as the 911's shape is its facia, little changed for the new Carrera. Major dials are easy to read but minor gauges get obscured. New heat/vent arrangements are a big improvement.

Boot is very small.

Lotus Esprit Turbo SE's 159mph. Nothing else at the price comes close, although, if Ferrari is to be believed, the more expensive 348 will see the far side of 160mph.

The Carrera 2 piles on performance ranking points when it comes to sprinting, though. Not even the super-lusty 3.6-litre boxer engine can twist the fat rear wheels fiercely enough for traction to be broken for more than a few metres, but that's no bad thing. The Carrera 2 judders painfully but effectively off the line to record 0-30mph in just 2.1secs and 60mph in a hair-raising 5.1secs, statistics undoubtedly helped by the now slick and astonishingly quick gearshift.

Only the savagely rapid Esprit Turbo SE has the measure of the Carrera 2 to 60mph with a time of 4.9secs. The Porsche still has its jaws locked firmly on the Esprit's tail at 100mph, recording a time of 12.7secs to the Lotus's 12.4secs. It's the Carrera, however, that covers the standing kilometre – perhaps the single most pertinent benchmark of ground-covering potential – more swiftly with a time of 24.6secs against the SE's 25.3secs, sharing a 132mph top speed.

The real beauty of the Porsche's engine is the sheer breadth of the power band and its scintillating kick above about 4000rpm. If it sometimes feels less than enthralling at modest revs, it's only because the final rush of revs to the 7000rpm red line is so devastating. It gives the Carrera 2's performance a delicious duplicity. The car can be driven with a level of laziness that borders on negligence, pulling crisply on a whiff of throttle from absurdly low revs in fourth or fifth.

But outstanding tractability soon becomes a solid shove in the back. Take a look at the fifth gear 30-50mph time of 7.5secs (11.2secs for the Esprit). Plant the accelerator in the carpet and the response is instant and relentless. The fourth gear 50-70mph time of 5.5secs is impressive by any standards but the 70-90 and 80-100mph times of 5.0 and 5.1secs respectively show how much the Porsche still has in hand.

Enhancing what must be close to the ultimate in user-friendly performance is the 911's inimitable and addictive chain-saw-in-cotton-wool engine note – that benign growl with a hint of distant menace. It doesn't sizzle and crackle in quite the same way as it used to but neither is it quite so loud, especially at speed. The aural enjoyment lasts all the longer as a result.

Not only is the gearchange as swift as the driver cares to make it but it's also beautifully well defined. The across-gate 2/3 action is a dream, the 4/5 movement less slick but still good. The clutch action, too, has been improved out of all recognition; it requires a meaty push but the tricky over-centre action has gone and take-up is very progressive. Only the gear ratios remain a bit odd – both long and widely spaced, though the engine does a marvellous job of filling the holes (something that was quite beyond the Turbo) and the 98mph third is a perfect overtaking gear.

Whether Porsche customers view economy as a prime consideration these days is open to interpretation, but they have usually done rather better than owners of rival supercars. The Carrera 2 continues the trend, our hard-driven test car returning 20.4mpg overall – remarkable in view of the performance. A projected touring consumption of 24.6mpg is also conspicuously good by class standards and permits a practical range of around 416 miles on a 16.9 gallon tankful of unleaded.

Handling and Ride

The 26-year-old amelioration of the 911's handling deficiencies reached its apogee with the Carrera 4 which, through sheer weight of technology, rushed tail slides precipitated merely by lifting off the throttle mid-bend out of existence.

That the Carrera 2 displays a similar disinclination to let go at the back is even more impressive, especially since it is paired with a sense of agility and adjustability seldom apparent in the C4. Seat of the pants inputs

Technical Focus

The Carrera 2's air cooled **flat-six engine** is identical to that in the C4 and, with 250bhp at 6100rpm, is the most powerful normally-aspirated 911 unit yet. Engine and gearbox are a single unit at the rear. Maximum torque of 210lb ft is developed at 4800rpm. Bore and stroke increases give **a swept volume of 3600cc.**

Twin plugs and dual ignition help keep combustion clean and, despite high 11.3:1 compression ratio, engine runs on unleaded. **Three-way catalytic converter** is standard for UK cars, making unleaded obligatory. Optional Tiptronic semi-automatic transmission allows clutchless manual shifting as well as fully automatic operation.

count for more in this car, but no longer are they the driver's only shot. Unlike previous 911s, the Carrera 2 is a fundamentally well balanced and stable machine.

Power assistance certainly hasn't harmed the 911's helm responses. It may have removed some of the more gratuitous feedback effects – the exaggerated writhing and kick-back – but what remains is more useful and married to perfect weighting and gearing. Given the massive grip of the Bridgestone RE71 tyres, the tight dimensions of the C2's body, fine visibility and the facility to administer big reserves of power with great accuracy and there can be no disputing this Porsche's immense stature as a superfast ground coverer.

That said, the driver who puts his wits on the back burner is still likely to singe his fingers with this car. It may be an easier 911 to drive quickly but it's still one in which you need to read the road accurately, especially if it's wet. The point at which the driver squeezes the throttle on the exit of a wet bend is critical. Too much too soon and the nose

runs wide; administer the gas late and the tail twitches disconcertingly before digging in and putting the fabulous traction to best use. Feeding in the power gradually is still the best way round,

On dry roads, however, the Carrera 2 is remarkably forgiving, not only resisting lift-off oversteer but also allowing the brakes to be applied deep into a bend to tuck the nose in towards the apex. Hard on the power again and the C2 catapults from the exit with the ferocity of a steam sled.

It's harder to be positive about this Porsche's ride. Put plainly, it's extremely firm and while suspension control is beyond criticism, its absorption properties are poor. The Porsche copes badly with humps and sudden camber changes and feels unpleasantly harsh over small irregularities. Worse still is its reaction to sharp ruts and cat's eyes. The suspension thumps over these so fiercely the result sounds like grapeshot fire. Road roar on coarse surfaces is just as poorly suppressed.

On the road, stopping power is unimpeachable, allied to a firm and meaty pedal feel.

At the Wheel

As recognisably '911' as the Carrera 2's external appearance, the cabin continues to mix good ideas with bad execution. Thus, the array of instruments is impressively comprehensive but only the centrally-sited revcounter is genuinely easy to read. Twelve new ing lights are a welcome addition nonetheless. As before, much of the minor switchgear comprises fiddly micro-switches located either on or underneath the facia. This isn't merely anti-ergonomic, it's a mess. The driving position isn't good, either. Despite the contribution of well-shaped seats that adjust for reach, rake, height and tilt to the whirring of electric motors, the fixed steering wheel and pedals that are heavily offset to the left impose compromises.

Comfort and Space

The Carrera 2 just about cuts it as a 2+2 in an emergency but is best treated as a two-seater — in which case both leg and headroom are fine and the backrests of the rear seats fold flat to provide a flat and stable luggage platform. It's just as well because you can't get much in the front boot, despite the minimal space occupied by the space-saver spare wheel.

The new heating and ventilation arrangements with their simple and easily understood controls are a huge improvement on the antiquated system of the old 911.

Finish and Equipment

Our test car came with the standard cloth-faced seats which looked rather ordinary in beige, though at least they harmonised well with the hues and materials employed throughout the rest of the cabin. This isn't always the case with Porsches. Build quality and detail finish were up to Porsche's usual impeccable standards.

Standard equipment includes ABS braking, a 10-speaker Blaupunkt stereo system and an ultrasonic alarm system that is automatically armed when the central locking is activated.

Verdict

One tester was moved to call the Carrera 2 inspired. Another opined that, despite its storming performance, less treacherous handling and unmistakable charisma, he couldn't live with one. The driving position, suspension harshness and road roar constituted problems he wasn't prepared to overlook.

So it seems that, 26 years on, the most famous sports car still in production continues to split opinion. Faster and fitter than ever, it simply has to be the best 911 to date by any objective reckoning. Yet it seems to be the

Summary

Performance	★★★★★★★★★☆
Economy	★★★★★★★★☆☆
Transmission	★★★★★★★★☆☆
Handling	★★★★★★★☆☆☆
Ride comfort	★★★☆☆☆☆☆☆☆
Brakes	★★★★★★★☆☆☆
Accommodation	★★★★★☆☆☆☆☆
Boot/storage	★★★★☆☆☆☆☆☆
At the wheel	★★★★☆☆☆☆☆☆
Visibility	★★★★★★★☆☆☆
Instruments	★★★★★★☆☆☆☆
Heating	★★★★★★★☆☆☆
Ventilation	★★★★★★★☆☆☆
Noise	★★★★★☆☆☆☆☆
Finish	★★★★★★★★★☆
Equipment	★★★★★★★★☆☆
OUR RATING	★★★★★★★★☆☆
VALUE RATING	★★★★★★★☆☆☆

perpetual Porsche's lot to be a flawed machine. Loyal Porsche customers will accommodate the shortcomings for the thrill of owning a car that, perhaps more than any other, continues to represent driving in its purest form. On the other hand, the Carrera 2 might not be the car to pull in extra business for Porsche.

CARRERA 4: HOW GOOD?

Reproduced from *Autocar & Motor*
6 December 1989

The Carrera 4 is, in some ways, a better car than the Carrera 2. On wet or slippery roads, the advantages are as clear cut as you might imagine: still better traction out of bends; more progressive and consistent steering responses when the road demands quick bursts of power; marginally higher levels of overall

THE PERFORMANCE STORY

TOP SPEED	Carrera 2 Mph	Carrera 4 Mph	ACCELERATION IN GEAR		
			Fourth gear	secs	secs
Mean	158	156	20–40	5.7	6.3
Best	160	159	30–50	5.4	5.8
			40–60	5.4	5.9
ACCELERATION FROM REST			59–70	5.5	5.9
mph	**secs**	**secs**	60–80	5.3	5.8
0–30	2.1	1.9	70–90	5.0	5.7
0–40	3.0	2.9	80–100	5.1	5.6
0–50	4.0	4.0	90–110	5.3	5.9
0–60	5.1	5.2	100–120	6.0	7.0
0–70	6.7	7.0	**Fifth gear**		
0–80	8.3	8.8	20–40	8.2	—
0–90	10.2	11.0	30–50	7.5	7.9
0–100	12.7	14.0	40–60	7.3	7.9
0–110	15.3	17.4	50–70	7.4	8.2
0–120	18.7	21.3	60–80	7.6	8.4
0–130	23.7	27.5	70–90	8.1	8.8
Standing			80–100	8.1	9.1
¼-mile:	13.6	13.9	90–110	7.7	9.2
Standing km:	24.6	25.5	100–120	8.2	9.9
30–70mph			110–130	8.2	9.7
through gears:	4.6	5.1	120–140	—	11.7

grip and a subliminal impression of enhanced stability and security as alien to ingrained 911 sensibilities as convenient switchgear.

And that's on merely wet roads. Drop the temperature below zero and the two cars become separate propositions. It's all much as you'd expect. The more interesting question, however, is what price all-weather ability?

It's a matter we went some way towards resolving in a previous issue when the two cars met head-to-head in Germany. On dry roads, the Carrera 4 driver feels a little more detached from the action than his C2 counterpart. Turn-in is slightly tardier, initial understeer stronger. In broad terms, the all-drive Porsche gives the impression of being a touch less agile – a sabre with a blunted edge.

The differences are easier to understand when you compare the two cars' weights: 1380kg for the C2, 1460kg for the C4 – a 5.7 per cent increase. Porsche claims that the C4's extra weight – and the power dissipation involved with driving all four wheels – is insignificant up to 60mph. The implication is that it is significant everywhere else and, save for top speed where the C2 is just 2mph faster at 158mph, this is precisely the case.

In fact, the C2 is a bare tenth quicker to 60mph than the C4 which returns 5.2 secs. Thereafter, the rear-drive Carrera gradually but inexorably pulls away to reach 100mph in 12.7secs (14.0secs for C4) and 130mph in a stunning 23.7secs (27.5secs). Remove the advantage afforded by the C4's superior traction off the line, however, and the Carrera 2 emerges as a clearly harder sprinter in the UK-legal band. Its 4.6secs through the gears 30-70mph time borders on the sensational, not only trouncing the C4's 5.1secs but shading the Lotus Esprit Turbo SE's 4.7secs.

The advantage lies with the Carrera 2 in 4th and 5th gear flexibility, too. Just compare the figures in the comparison table.

Appendix

PORSCHE CLUBS – INTERNATIONAL DIRECTORY

Porsche Club Great Britain
Executive Director: Roy Gillham,
Ayrton House,
West End,
Northleach,
Gloucestershire GL54 3HG,
Great Britain

Porsche Club of America
Secretary: Sandi Misura,
1753 Las Gallina,
San Rafael,
California 94903,
USA

Porsche Club Argentina
Secretary: David Santana,
Avenida Santa Fe 950,
1640 Acussuso,
Buenos Aires,
Argentina

Porsche Club of New South Wales
Secretary: John Clark,
PO Box 183,
Lindfield NSW 2070,
Australia

Porsche Club of Western Australia
Secretary: Rob Jones,
PO Box 447,
South Perth,
Western Australia 6151,
Australia

Austria: Porsche Club Wien
Secretary: Ing Udo Poeschmann,
Mariahilfer Str 19–21,
A-1060 Vienna,
Austria

Porsche Club Belgique
50 rue du Mail,
B-1050,
Brussels,
Belgium

Porsche Club of Brazil
Secretary: Claudio Tozzi,
Rua Nigeria 121,
BR-04538 Sao Paulo,
Brazil

Porsche Club Denmark
Secretary: Flemming L Nielsem,
Ved Jaegerdiget 9A,
DK-2670 Greye Strand,
Denmark

Porsche Club Deutschland
Secretary: Manfred Pfeiffer,
Podbielskiallee 25–27,
D-1000 Berlin 33,
West Germany

Porsche Club Suomi-Finland
Secretary: Klaus Kingelin,
Sipilan Kartano,
SF-12380 Lappakoski,
Finland

Porsche Club de France
Secretary: Marc Tripels,
c/o Sonauto SA,
1 Avenue de Fief,
BP 479,
F-95005 Cergy Pontoise Cedex,
France

Porsche Club Holland
Secretary: P Polle,
Wim Sonneveldlaan 227,
NL-3584 ZS Utrecht,
Netherlands

Porsche Club Hong Kong
Secretary: Wong Chuk Hang,
No 1 Yip Fat Street,
PO Box 24539,
Aberdeen Post Office,
Aberdeen,
Hong Kong

Porsche Club Italia
Secretary: Gabriella Bigontina,
Via Carlo Osma 2,
I-201151 Milano,
Italy

Porsche Club of Japan
Secretary: H Sumitani,
c/o Mitsuwa Motor Co Ltd,
No 18–6 Roppongi 3-Chome,
Miniato-Ku,
Tokyo 106,
Japan

Porsche Club Luxembourg
Secretary: J Frast,
c/o Novotel,
E42-route d'Echternach,
L-1453 Luxembourg-Dommeldang
Luxembourg

Nederlandse Porsche Club
Van Alkemadelaan 878,
Den Haag,
Netherlands

Porsche Club of New Zealand
Secretary: J Robertson,
204 Beach Road,
Campbell's Bay,
Auckland,
New Zealand

Porsche Club Norway
Secretary: Johannes Bidesbol,
Postboks 32,
Lysejordet,
N-Oslo 7,
Norway

Porsche Club of South Africa
Secretary: Angela Hauser,
PO Box 9834,
Johannesburg 2000,
South Africa

Porsche Club Spain
Secretary: Immaculada Sanz,
Paseo de la Castellana 240,
Madrid 16,
Spain

Porsche Club Sweden
Secretary: Stina Liljeberg,
Postbox 340 25,
S-10026 Stockholm,
Sweden

Porsche Club Romand
Secretary: Philippe Collet,
Chateau 13,
CH-18-6 St Legier,
Switzerland

Porsche Club Zurich
Secretary: Roland Studer,
c/o Oscar Senn-Bucher,
Boldistrasse 76,
CH-5414 Rieden/Bussbaumen,
Switzerland

Index